James Joyce's
A PORTRAIT OF THE ARTIST AS A YOUNG MAN

A CRITICAL COMMENTARY

W9-BTF-131

EDWARD A. KOPPER, JR.
PROFESSOR OF ENGLISH
SLIPPERY ROCK STATE COLLEGE

MONARCH PRESS

Published by
MONARCH PRESS
a division of Simon & Schuster, Inc.
a Gulf+Western Company
1 West 39th Street
New York, N.Y. 10018

Standard Book Number: 671-00563-4

Printed in the United States of America

A NOTE TO THE STUDENT

In this Monarch Note, Professor Edward A. Kopper, Jr., seeks to enhance your understanding and enjoyment of James Joyce's *A Portrait of the Artist as a Young Man*. However, his critical commentary will have little value for you unless you are already familiar with the novel itself. Doctor Kopper assumes throughout his discussion that it will prompt you to refer back continually to the original text.

—THE EDITORS

TABLE OF CONTENTS

JOYCE'S LIFE AND WORKS

LIFE

James Joyce was born on February 2, 1882 in Rathgar, a suburb near Dublin; and, in 1887, the family moved to Bray (the setting for the Christmas Dinner scene in *A Potrait*), another suburb of Dublin. In September 1888, Joyce was enrolled in Clongowes Wood College, operated by the Jesuits, located about twenty miles west of Dublin. In June 1891, Joyce was withdrawn from Clongowes after his father, John Joyce, lost his position as tax collector for Dublin. In 1891, too, Joyce wrote "Et Tu, Healy!", commemorating the demise of Parnell.

In 1892, the family moved to Blackrock, between Dublin and Bray, but, because of financial insolvency, relocated to Dublin in 1893. Joyce attended the Christian Brothers school in North Richmond Street—a source for "Araby"—and then, in April, was enrolled in Belvedere College, conducted by the Jesuits. In February 1894, Joyce travelled with his father to Cork to sell the remaining family property.

In 1895, Joyce joined the Sodality of the Blessed Virgin Mary and, in 1896, was elected to the prestigious post of Sodality Prefect. He was re-elected to the position in 1897 and, in 1898, underwent the rigors of the famous Retreat in honor of St. Francis Xavier. Joyce graduated from Belvedere in 1898 and entered University College, Dublin.

At college, Joyce refused to sign the protest against Yeats's *The Countess Cathleen* in 1899; in 1900, he delivered his essay, *Drama and Life,* which divorced art from explicit moral themes, before the university's Literary and Historical Society; he published, in the same year, a favorable commentary on Ibsen in the *Fortnightly Review;* and, in 1901, he penned *The Day of the Rabblement,* which attacked the Irish Literary Theatre.

In 1902, already an advanced student of linguistics, Joyce received his degree in modern languages from University College, Dublin, left for Paris to study medicine and, in 1903, was called home by the message that his mother was dying. In 1904, he lived in the Martello Tower in Sandymount with Oliver Gogarty and, on June 10, met Nora Barnacle—his father told him: "She'll stick to you." In October, Joyce travelled with her to Paris, Zurich, Trieste, and Pola, where he began to teach at the Berlitz School. Joyce's stay in the Martello Tower became the source for the first chapter of *Ulysses*, "Telemachus"; and all of the events in that novel take place on June 16, 1904, "Bloomsday"—possibly the day on which Joyce fell in love with Nora. In 1904, too, Joyce's essay, "A Portrait of the Artist," was rejected by *Dana,* and he began to rewrite it as *Stephen Hero* (though some commentators maintain that Joyce began to make notes for what became *Stephen Hero* as early as 1901).

In 1905, Joyce moved to Trieste, where his son, Giorgio, was born on July 27; in 1906, he moved to Rome, where he worked in a bank; and, in 1907, Joyce returned to Trieste, where he became a tutor of English. His daughter, Lucia, was born on July 26, 1907. In that year, Joyce wrote "The Dead" and, in September, began to rework the twenty-six chapters of *Stephen Hero* into the five lengthy sections of *A Portrait of the Artist as a Young Man.* In 1911, discouraged by his failure to have *Dubliners* published, he flung the manuscript of *A Portrait* into the fire—fortunately, his sister, Eileen, was nearby and snatched it out. In 1912, Joyce made his last trip to Ireland.

In 1914, *A Portrait* was published in serial form by *The Egoist,* and *Dubliners* by Grant Richards. In 1915, living in Zurich, Joyce completed *Exiles.* He then began to receive a number of subsidies to continue writing, his most important sponsor being Harriet Shaw Weaver. In 1917, he underwent his first eye surgery for a condition that was to plague him throughout his life, leaving him nearly sightless, though not blind.

In 1918, the *Little Review* (New York) began to publish *Ulysses* in serial form but, in 1920, was enjoined to cease doing so on a complaint by the Society for the Prevention of Vice. In 1920, too, Joyce met Ezra Pound and moved with his family to Paris. In 1922, *Ulysses* was published in Paris, on Joyce's birthday, by Sylvia Beach's Shakespeare and Company.

In 1923, Joyce began *Finnegans Wake* and saw the work through the press serially, as *Work in Progress,* in the *Transatlantic Review* and then in *transition.* During this time, *Ulysses* was being pirated in the United States since the government regarded the novel as obscene and would not grant Joyce copyright privileges.

In 1931, on July 4, Joyce and Nora were married; his father died on December 29. In 1932, Joyce wrote the brief "Ecce Puer," a poem celebrating the birth of his grandson to Giorgio and Helen Joyce, and Lucia was diagnosed as schizophrenic. She was to remain institutionalized. In 1933, Judge John Woolsey ruled that *Ulysses* was not pornographic, and, in 1934, the novel was published by Random House. In 1936, the *Collected Poems* was issued and, in 1939, *Finnegans Wake.*

Joyce died on January 13, 1941, in Zurich, where he was forced to go (leaving Lucia behind) to escape the outbreak of war.

Three great influences upon Joyce's writing are music, including the popular lyrics of Ireland; Roman Catholicism, which he could never quite break away from psychologically; and the political skirmishes of his youth, which helped confirm his belief in his role as exile.

MAJOR WORKS

Dubliners, 1914. This collection of short stories describes what Joyce saw as the "moral paralysis" of a nation: its bewitchment by the clergy and its bondage to both English tyranny and to its own sense of the past. Although Joyce's model in the Naturalistic sketches is not so much Thomas Moore as Ibsen, recent critics have found a great deal of abstruse symbolism in Joyce's eminently realistic details.

Some of the more famous stories in *Dubliners* include "The Sisters," in which a young boy is initiated into the world of repressive Dublin Catholicism at the wake of a priest; "Clay," which demonstrates how an otherwise vibrant woman has been turned into lifeless clay by her sterile Dublin environment; and "Ivy Day in the Committee Room," which contrasts modern politicians, with their mercenary practicality, to the dead hero, Parnell.

A great deal of exegesis has been afforded "Araby" and "The Dead." In the former, a young lad tries to objectify his imaginative longing for an idealized love by going to a bazaar to buy his beloved a gift—when he arrives, most of the lights of the fair are out; and, through an overheard conversation, he realizes that his emotions have misled him. "The Dead" delineates both the deadness of Ireland, with its ceaseless chatter about past glories, and the dearth of passion in the protagonist, Gabriel Conroy, who comes to see that he has never experienced the passion which (he learns) led Michael Furey to "die for" Gabriel's wife, Gretta, when she and Furey were youngsters.

One large theme in *Dubliners* is simony, the buying and selling of sacred things: Joyce feels that Dubliners have given up their birthright of freedom for the guarantees of middle-class security and a Heaven after death.

Ulysses, 1922. In this lengthy and intricate novel, Joyce bases the peregrinations of Leopold Bloom across Dublin upon the wanderings of Odysseus; Bloom is the most elaborately developed character in fiction. Although Stephen Dedalus appears frequently in *Ulysses*, Joyce is more interested in his lower-middle-class advertising canvasser than in his bright young man.

Great debates ensue among Joyceans as to whether Bloom is "saint" or "sinner" — or neither. More important is that Joyce changed his Greek source considerably to create in Bloom a man of compassion: Odysseus destroys his wife's suitors; but Bloom, returning home, tries to accommodate himself to his unfaithful Molly.

Ulysses is mock-heroic, comically contrasting Bloom's inability (and unwillingness) to change his destiny with Odysseus' hawkish attitudes; but the novel also reveals the great worth to be found in this anti-hero, this "common man." Ironically, some Marxist critics are dissuaded by this great proletariat document, feeling that its baroque art manifests a decadent western civilization.

In the final stages of *Ulysses,* Stephen meets Bloom— the "son" finds his "father," as in *The Odyssey*—but rejects Bloom's offer of a lodging for the night, preferring to wander off alone.

Finnegans Wake, 1939. In this massive and complex work, Stephen becomes Shem, the symbol of the writer who uses his own intestines to spin out his works. Although heroic when compared with his charlatan brother, Shaun, Shem is treated with irony throughout the book, as Joyce seems to be bidding a final (and belated) goodbye to his youth. H.C. Earwicker, the pubkeeper whose "dream" takes up the 628 pages of multi-lingual puns, is another outsider (like Bloom), a Dane and Protestant living in a Catholic country.

If the "answer" to life presented in *A Portrait* is intellect; and, in *Ulysses,* love; then *Finnegans Wake* implies that energy is paramount: a willing acceptance of the new day, while knowing that it will be no better than the last. In *Finnegans Wake,* Joyce's almost incredibly intricate architectonics structure an ironically simple theme: life is lived best in the small happenings of every day.

Two Lesser Works. *Exiles,* a play published in 1918, has never been successful on the stage. Written in the manner of Ibsen (but without his offsetting humor), it is Joyce's self-dramatization of many issues that perplexed him, including the role of the artist in society and the protagonist's need for the total love of his mate, coupled with his belief that she must be free to choose her own emotional attachments. As with *Chamber Music*, it is interesting to read *Exiles* in relation to Joyce's other works.

Chamber Music, published in 1907, is a collection of often vague poems, but it does contain, in embryonic form, several themes later developed by Joyce.

"Stephen Hero" as Source for "A Portrait."

We can appreciate *A Portrait* better by seeing the use that Joyce made of this ur-work, *Stephen Hero*, in writing the later novel. Also, *Stephen Hero* provides a good deal of material which is helpful in understanding Stephen's motivations in *A Portrait*. Critics have compared reading *Stephen Hero* to looking into a room with the door wide open; in *A Portrait*, we peer through a keyhole.

Joyce compressed radically events and characters from *Stephen Hero* in writing *A Portrait*—and sometimes excised them altogether. The earlier work describes the death of Isabel, Stephen's sister, who doesn't appear in *A Portrait;* includes Mr. Fulham, Stephen's godfather, who discusses Mr. Tate, Stephen's English teacher, with the lad; develops the character of Maurice, Stephen's younger brother, who at one point comments, in a balanced way, upon a retreat sermon: "Usual kind of thing. Stink in the morning and pain of loss in the evening"; and revives the ill-natured Wells as a seminarian. Typically, then, events become increasingly sinister in *A Portrait* as the focus is more narrowly placed on Stephen's emotions and spirit and as much greater emphasis is given to the suggestiveness of details.

It is interesting, too, to discover in *Stephen Hero* that Stephen referred to Emma as Miss Clery, and to be told explicitly that his aesthetic theories were influenced by Ibsen, Blake, and Rimbaud, the last helping to account for his love of words, evidenced at the end of the fourth chapter in *A Portrait*. In the later novel, Joyce underplays Stephen's reliance upon "sources" for his ideas, especially during the illumination scene with the bird-girl.

Other differences between *Stephen Hero* and *A Portrait* include Stephen's use of a prepared format to present his aesthetic theory, which is outlined cryptically to Lynch in Chapter Five of *A Portrait;* and Joyce's simplifying of Stephen's last name, *"Daedalus."* Finally, Joyce changed the title of the book, *Stephen Hero,* feeling that it was too heavily ironic.

STRUCTURAL DEVICES IN "A PORTRAIT"

The Title. The title of Joyce's novel is a key to his intention in *A Portrait*. It is "a" portrait, one of many that could have been painted: the novel focuses upon the growth of the protagonist's mind, pursuing in a labyrinthine but progressive manner his quest for the liberated condition of the incipient artist. Also, since Stephen is to become an "artist," it is mandatory that his tale be told pictorially, that the reader perceive the wholeness of Joyce's vision. Thus Joyce's novel underplays traditional chronological order, except as a loose means of presenting his hero to the audience; instead, Joyce unifies his narrative by devices common to painting (and music): motifs and symbols.

As Joyce often stressed, the last four words of the title must be emphasized. Stephen, at the conclusion of the book, is still somewhat ingenuous, still inflated by his own self-importance. Also, the connotation of "artist," in Joyce's time a "character," helps to account for Joyce's irony in the later stages of *A Portrait*. Finally, *A Portrait* is both a *Bildungseroman*, a novel of education or initiation, and a *Künstlerroman*, one which concerns the development of an artist.

Growth of Stephen's Personality. Stephen's personality is developed through a series of contrasts between his "high" moments and his "low" moments. The most important of these occur at the ends and beginnings of chapters, but many scenes within the individual chapters are balanced and counterpointed, as well. In Chapter One, Stephen's punishment by Dolan, in which he is temporarily "blinded" by tears, contrasts with the end of the chapter, in which he is exalted by classmates following his successfull petition to Conmee. At the start of Chapter Two, Stephen's temporary éclat is lost as the scene shifts to his impoverished family, with Uncle Charles sitting in the outhouse. Chapter Two ends with Stephen swooning into the arms of the prostitute, and Chapter Three shows him buried in self-reproach. The exhilaration which Stephen feels after his Confession and reception of Communion at the conclusion of Chapter Three is lost in the nitpicking logic of his conversion at the start of Chapter Four. Chapter Four ends in Stephen's beatification by the bird-girl, but the beginning of Chapter Five finds him mired once again in his dishevelled household. Chapter Five ends with Stephen looking forward to a new life abroad; and, as Stephen calls upon Daedalus to assist him in his search, Joyce suggests that perhaps his future "deflation" will not be so great—he has now left behind, at least physically, the forces which have hampered him from the start of *A Portrait*.

Besides lending the novel artistic unity, the balanced episodes fit into the "bird imagery" of *A Portrait*: Stephen's successes are all short flights, meant to prepare him for his final voyage to artistic integrity. They also blend with the water imagery of the novel, describing as they do the ebbs and flows of Stephen's emotional growth.

Joyce's use of contrast within a chapter is seen best in Chapter Two. The flashback to his defense of Byron occurs when he is preparing to act the part of "farcical pedagogue" in the school play; his love poetry to Emma, divorced from crass reality, culminates in the stark physiology of his visit to the prostitute, who becomes Mother Church in Chapter Three. The word "Foetus," which he sees in the anatomy theatre, leads to no immediate rebirth, but begins the cycle of false security, guilt, and more false security.

The contrasting scenes, besides depicting realistically the growth of most people's psyches, broach the theme of history repeating itself—a concept which Joyce developed at length in *Finnegans Wake*, using ideas from the Neapolitan historian, Vico. Finally, on a psychological level, Stephen's ups and downs lead one to wonder if he will ever be able to incorporate the material of "real life" into a plausible view of the universe.

Epiphanies. Between 1900 and 1903, Joyce wrote a number of short pieces which he termed "epiphanies," brief revelations of character, gleaned from otherwise trivial and casual moments. Using an even more emphatic Biblical analogy, Joyce termed such perceptions "eucharistic." The word "Epiphany" of course refers to the illumination bestowed upon the Wise Men when they were permitted to know that the Infant Christ was actually God. Joyce abandoned the formal use of the term in *A Portrait;* but, as will be shown, several critics have not been content to let it drop. The older Joyce saw through the pretentious plan of his youth, to send the epiphanies to all the great libraries of the world in the event of his death; and, in *Ulysses,* he has Stephen muse wistfully upon his juvenile intention to donate to Alexandria his "epiphanies on green oval leaves, deeply deep. . . ."

Whether one believes that an epiphanic structure underlies *A Portrait* or not, it is useful to see the novel in terms of the illuminations that Stephen experiences on his journey away from the teachings of his youth.

False Father Theme. The priests in *A Portrait* are a mixed lot: Conmee and the Director, for example, demonstrate some shrewdness; Dolan and Arnall, on the other hand, are inadequate—and the old Capuchin to whom Stephen confesses tries to help but is buried under centuries of worthless religious formalism. Joyce's priests are, for the most part, "false fathers": the description of Dolan during the pandying episode fills in the face of Simon Dedalus, which was merely sketched on the first page of the book—both tell Stephen fairy tales, and at Clongowes, Stephen is punished for not doing his lesson in Latin, the language through which the fairy tale of Roman Catholicism is promulgated.

These false clerical fathers, it is hinted, might be less than masculine, though, once again, we see them through Stephen's point-of-view: one priest simpers over Bertie Tallon's female clothing on the night of Stephen's play, and the Director criticizes the Capuchins for wearing "skirts," apparently convinced that his less bizarre cassock is not womanish. They are sinister figures, as well: the punishment that they will administer to Corrigan is spoken of in hushed tones; Conmee's office is musty, and a skull rests on his desk; Father Arnall, during the infamous Retreat Sermon, is not speaking so much of a theological Hell, but of his personal, living Inferno, and his picture of the avenging Godhead could almost have come from de Sade; and the Director tries to ensnare Stephen with his offer of secret knowledge should he be ordained and to determine subtly whether the externally holy lad is worthy of Holy Orders.

Joyce comments at such length upon the priests not merely to satirize the clergy but to demonstrate the strength of the forces that Stephen must break free from. As the novel progresses, Stephen does come to see his "fathers" not so much as all-powerful emissaries of God, but as trite servants of a half-understood creed. He perceives them no longer so much as soldiers of Christ but as camp followers. Though Stephen's attitude towards the priests in the second half of the novel is condescending, it is also more mature than his views of them up until the discussion of his vocation in Chapter Four. After this confrontation, Stephen sees mainly their banality and sterility, although he does experience occasional feelings of hatred for them, especially for Father Moran, who remains off stage.

But in all of this, one might ask, as does Father Noon, what would have happened to Stephen if he had had to undergo the rigors of, for example, an English public school?

Characterizing the priests as he does, Joyce has in mind the well-known song, "The Croppy Boy," written by Malone during the nineteenth century. This lachrymose ballad, which is quoted throughout *Ulysses*, tells of a farm boy who is going off to war to follow in the footsteps of his father and brothers, all of whom have been killed fighting the British. He stops to have his confession heard; and, after Father Green has listened to the childish recital of trivial offenses, he throws off his cassock and reveals himself to be a British captain. The Croppy Boy is hanged at Geneva Barrack. Father Green, then, becomes the prototype in Joyce's work of the "false father," the Englishman (or the priest) who usurps the little green place called Ireland.

Meals: Eucharistic and Not. Resembling Kafka's Hunger Artist, Stephen often refuses to or is unable to eat the food of society that is prepared for him. He divorces himself from the sounds of Clongowes' refectory; he cannot eat the sustenance served by his mother during the abortive Christmas Dinner, and later she announces her intention to pray for her son's return to Communion and the faith; and Stephen is offered food by his father when the protagonist learns in Chapter Two that his courageous complaint to Father Conmee was really considered a joke by the priests involved. At that time, Simon praises the Jesuits for their fine tables and decides to send his son to Belvedere, a school conducted by such cosmopolitan priests.

When Stephen does eat fully, the circumstances suggest that his "appetite" is misdirected: before the retreat, he is lost in what he considers serious sins, among them gluttony; and, after his confession, he joins with his fellows to receive the Eucharist, looking forward all the time to the large meal at home which will follow Mass.

Stephen pictures himself rejecting the "grapes" proffered by Mercedes, and it is not until he decides to become a priest of the imagination, transforming the bread of common moments into the Eucharist of art, that he begins to define his relationship with the food of life. Joyce spells "Mass" in lower case throughout A Portrait to suggest that Stephen will not accept what is satisfying to the mass of people: he will create his own Mass after leaving Ireland.

The Myth of Daedalus. Stephen's namesake, the Greek Daedalus, built the labyrinth for the minotaur in Crete, and Joyce patterns Stephen's personality upon several aspects of his "ancestor." Just as Daedalus was an architect, so Stephen will be a builder in words. Daedalus was a social critic; Stephen insists upon his rights to challenge all creeds. Most important, Daedalus was able to fly out of the labyrinth—which was so complex that even he, who designed it, could not pick his way back to the surface—by designing wings for his son, Icarus, and for himself. Icarus flew too close to the sun, despite the warnings of his father, and, the wings melting, dropped into the sea.

Stephen must find his way through the labyrinth of faith, family, and fatherland, and then must escape the "nets" that may be thrown over his ascending figure—but he must not be burned up in his emotions.

From the start of *A Portrait,* Stephen wonders if he is the son of Simon Dedalus or of the Greek Daedalus. He imagines seeing the winged form of his mythical forebear soaring in the air over Ireland as he is led towards his near "Baptism" at the end of Chapter Four; and, in the last sentence of the novel, Stephen calls upon Daedalus to be his spiritual companion during the European sojourn.

EMMA. Joyce employs Emma, an ordinary, somewhat flirtatious Catholic girl, to define Stephen's changing attitudes towards sex, religion, and womanhood. Emma is not a developed character and exists in *A Portrait* primarily so that Joyce might describe Stephen's evolving personality in relation to a member of the opposite sex. The presence of Emma permits us to experience Stephen's shyness in refusing to kiss her; his adolescent poetry, written to her, which unabashedly combines beginning sexual feelings with religious mottoes; and his loss of grace (wherein we discover that Stephen has been enjoying Emma in the corner of his mind), with the consequent need to regain blissful innocence. Stephen's relationship with Emma becomes more human in Chapter Five, when she serves as catalyst for his jealousy.

BIRDS. Joyce's use of bird imagery in the novel, though often contrived, reinforces the Daedalian patterns in *A Portrait*. If Stephen is to fly high and alone, he must soar above the Herons and Crane-lies and must cope with eagles such as Dante's retributive specters. In Chapter Five, the birds hovering near the National Library augur Stephen's role of mock prophet, after his illumination by the birdgirl; but, at the close of the novel, Stephen is still unable to cage the skittery bird, Emma. Birds throughout *A Por-*

trait suggest Stephen's flight from the middle class, with its materialistic concerns; and Joyce himself often wished to experience the freedom of the bird's unpremeditated song—ironic, in a writer whose work was so painstakingly structured.

WATER. Allusions to water in *A Portrait* denote the unpleasant aspects of Stephen's physical and spiritual environment, forces of which he must cleanse himself. Some of these include his bed-wetting; sewers and ditches, with foul water; Holy Water sprinkled by Uncle Charles, some of which (symbolically) misses Stephen; the tears of Stephen's mother, suggesting his bondage to the family; Stephen's hatred of washing; the waters of Sanctifying Grace, which temporarily purify his soul at the close of the Retreat; and swimming youngsters whom he avoids on his road to the bird-girl. This Pagan Mary, standing in the water, and Daedalus, flying above the waves, suggest that, eventually, Stephen will follow their lead, though in *A Portrait* his toes are still at the edge of the sea.

DEATH. Stephen dies emotionally several times in *A Portrait*, and it is only when he resolves to become an exile that life unblenchingly beckons to him; all other "rebirths" in the novel have been false starts. The deaths which he undergoes include his imagined passing in the infirmary at Clongowes, when he thinks of Parnell's demise; his feeling that his life has ended while he is in Cork with his father; his belief during the Retreat that God is calling to him; and his conviction that his annihilation will mean little to God, as he attempts to mortify his flesh after his Communion at the end of Chapter Three.

THE MAJOR PROBLEM IN "A PORTRAIT":
JOYCE'S USE OF IRONY

THE DIFFICULTY. A valid interpretation of *A Portrait* rests upon one element, above all others: Joyce's use of irony in his characterization of Stephen Dedalus. *Once the reader is "clued in" to the fact that Joyce is not always sympathetic to Stephen, "tipped off" to Joyce's sometimes cruel satirizing of Stephen's aspirations, he must read the novel in a different light.*

Several questions, then, arise from Joyce's use of irony: When is Stephen being treated with sarcasm? When is Joyce unintentionally presenting Stephen ironically, i.e., when (if ever) does Joyce himself become so involved with his subject that he loses objectivity? And, most important of all, what are we to think of the total Stephen?

The problem of irony in *A Portrait*, then, is threefold: to assess Joyce's intentions in the work, to establish how well he succeeds in carrying them out, and to determine whether the effort of writing about Stephen was worth the trouble—Is Stephen heroic merely by comparison with the turgid and timid people surrounding him? Another complication arises when we try to define the *degree* of irony with which Stephen is treated in each of the episodes.

DIVERGING VIEWS. Several views have been advanced during the last twenty years of Joycean criticism to define Joyce's attitude towards Stephen. Hugh Kenner represents those who have come to be called (glibly) Stephen-haters: he finds Stephen, especially the aesthetic Stephen of the last chapter, unlikable and somewhat shallow. Other critics feel that Joyce is basically on the side of Stephen throughout the entire *Portrait*. A third school of critics feels that it does not really matter whether we define Joyce's intentions regarding Stephen; the novel, these critics believe, exists as it is and speaks to the individual reader.

15

A fourth, more subtle, position holds that there is no inherent contradiction in seeing Stephen as both heroic and farcical *at the same time*. Influenced perhaps by the blending of comic and tragic elements in Joyce's later two works, critics of the fourth school find this same Brunonian commingling of opposites in *A Portrait*. A final eclectic approach tries to locate irony where it exists; it sees Stephen as a composite creature, composed of virtues and vices, and lets the matter of Joyce's intention remain a mixed bag.

In all of this, it is important to weigh the prejudices that we ourselves bring to *A Portrait*. Stephen became quite popular in the sixties as many social activists, ignoring his stridently apolitical and asocial nature, found in him a model of a rebel with whom college students could readily identify. On the other hand, more traditional professors, especially during the fifties, found intolerable Stephen's posturings at the university in Chapter Five of the novel. Also, many have been dissuaded by Stephen's "conversion" to art because of their own reactions against Pater, Newman, and Shelley. And many critics, influenced by sensitivity sessions and the need to "communicate," have excoriated Stephen's false pride, which prohibits him from really speaking to and listening to others. Thus, in many cases, critics have projected upon Joyce concepts that he could not have been aware of.

Though much recent criticism of *A Portrait* has been more valuable than early studies which ruminated at length upon Cranly's bird name and the identity of Eileen Vance, the body of Joyce scholarship has still not come close to defining Stephen's worth. The verdict is still out, and perhaps the results will never be satisfying. Viewed optimistically, the ambiguity surrounding Stephen's character is not unique in great literature. Critics are as yet unable to state exactly what Melville thought of Ahab, Shakespeare of Hamlet, and Christ, of Himself, in His sometimes ironic parables. In *A Portrait*, however, the search for an answer is far more important than it is in, for example, Henry James' *The Turn of the Screw*, with its endless questioning of whether the ghosts were real.

FURTHER REFLECTIONS ON "A PORTRAIT". We must realize, too, that *A Portrait,* although a great novel, is an early work of Joyce and not of the stature of *Ulysses* or *Finnegans Wake.* Joyce was an ardently careful writer, but not always, especially in *A Portrait,* an unblemished one. Sometimes he seems to tire of Stephen, and he evidences this fatigue by virtually dropping him as a serious person in *Ulysses;* at times, Joyce used *A Portrait* to purge his own residual hatred of the forces that almost destroyed both him and Stephen; and sometimes, too, Joyce expresses a small romantic part of himself that escaped through the net of his tight architectonics.

It is crucial that the reader not be defensive about *A Portrait.* No other "classic" is perfect, and *A Portrait* need not be without flaws. One is reminded of Percy Lubbock's observation that *War and Peace,* though a profound novel, would have been even better had Tolstoi employed more strictly Flaubertian point-of-view techniques. Thus it is a truism to contrast D.H. Lawrence's *Sons and Lovers,* which he admittedly wrote as a self-administered cathartic, saying that it "slipped unwatched" out of his pen, with the "cold" and "impersonal" *Portrait.* However, perhaps more could be gained by tracing similarities between the two books.

EVIDENCE OF INTENT. In defining Joyce's intention in *A Portrait,* we have access, as with other "classics," to external and internal evidence. The beginning student of *A Portrait* is well-advised to turn to Joyce's *Letters* (edited by Stuart Gilbert and Richard Ellmann), to Ellmann's definitive biography, *James Joyce,* and to the Robert Scholes and Richard M. Kain compilation of sources for the novel, *The Workshop of Daedalus.* Internal evidence, as will be seen later, examines such hints of intent as the changing linguistic and stylistic patterns which mark contrasting and balancing scenes in *A Portrait.*

SPECIFIC EXAMPLES OF IRONY. Generally, Joyce's irony increases as *A Portrait* progresses. With the possible exception of Stephen's vision of the bird-girl and with the even more tenuously possible exception of his composing the villanelle, Stephen is treated with detachment starting with his discussion of a vocation with the Director in Chapter Four. Joyce may feel that Stephen has now attained enough knowledge of the sly ways of the world to permit him to suffer the corrective of heavy irony without being annihilated by Joyce's sarcasm. Stephen has come through his reconversion to Catholicism and apparently has emerged as a fuller person. Unfortunately, Joyce does not show us how Stephen has overcome his scrupulous adherence to the mechanics of religion following reception of Communion at the end of Chapter Three. There is the suggestion that Stephen has merely replaced his scrupulous attitudes towards religion with equally scrupulous (and equally insubstantial) attitudes towards art.

Joyce suggests the reasons that Stephen leaves the Church but does not explain what he is escaping into. It is significant that his final vision is one of flight away from the realities that he knows best. The reader applauds the courage of Stephen's plunge but finds no evidence that he will create anything worthwhile in the future—and, in *Ulysses,* he still finds no evidence of the incipient artist. Even though Joyce, in his novel, deals with the artist *as a young man*, he may yet be at fault in not providing any data to show that Stephen will become an "artist" at all.

IRONIC RELIGIOUS SYMBOLISM. Joyce does little to appease the Stephenhaters when he compares the protagonist throughout *A Portrait* to Christ and to other religious figures. The argument over Parnell occurs during Stephen's first Christmas dinner with the family; he is mistreated by Dolan during Lent and "crucified" by Heron because of his defense of Byron; he acts in a Pentecost play and then sniffs the odor of horses' urine to still his emotions; he regards his visits to prostitutes as consecrations of Black Masses; and he becomes the Pharisee turned Publican as he awaits his shriving by the Capuchin. Stephen is baptized in the "Jordan" and Resurrected at the end of Chapter Four, officiates at Holy Week services during Chapter Five, and preaches his Gospel throughout the rest of the final chapter, aided by Cranly, his John the Baptist or Precursor.

Although he is "rejected" by his own people—or does Stephen reject them?—Stephen shares little of Christ's humanity or openness; and there is little in the novel which describes the effects of Stephen's rebirth. Bluntly speaking, the Christocentric symbolism in *A Portrait* stems in part from Joyce's own feelings of persecution. In no other set of symbols is the difference between Joyce and Stephen more clearly seen. In most essential ways, Stephen Dedalus is simply not James Joyce, and Joyce may well have realized this about two-thirds the way through *A Portrait*.

Stephen finds nothing to replace his forsaken God, and Father Noon is probably correct in maintaining that "art," in the best of times, is not religion.

PROBLEMS IN CHAPTER FIVE. Students of *A Portrait* are justified to some extent in not finding much of interest in the final (and longest) section. As the newly ordained priest of art, Stephen must preach his Gospel, and the fifth chapter of *A Portrait* is probably Joyce's addition to the Four Gospels of the New Testament; yet, Stephen's aesthetic theories, though they reveal a nimble mind, leave us cold. Perhaps the novel never recovers from the sentimental but moving tones of the end of Chapter Four. Possibly, too, Stephen's theories are meant to be an ironic self-commentary (not perceived by Stephen) upon the protagonist's belief that the presence of the artist should not be felt in the greatest of art: Stephen is eminently present in Chapter Five, and his didactics contrast sharply with his view that the artist must be refined out of existence. This view, in itself, is a tired application of Deism to artistic creation. Finally, the villanelle is a clever bit of writing and does incorporate Stephen's new, sacramental vision of human emotion—but, once again, its object, Emma Clery, does not seem worthy of all the attention. Or perhaps the object of the vision is Stephen himself.

To criticize Stephen thusly is not to throw out the baby with the wash water, for in many ways Stephen is heroic. We sympathize with his courageous opposition to the repressive force of Father Dolan; admire the uncompromising way in which he defends Byron and pursues his dream of beauty amidst the squalor of Dublin and, later, among inattentive fellow college students; we are uplifted by his youthful decision to leave his faith and country, though he fears the consequences; and, by seeing the exquisite sensitivity of his character, we realize how hard it is for Stephen to make the admirable decisions that he does arrive at by the end of the novel. It is regrettable that often we are more inclined to identify with Stephen's failures than with his successes.

TEXTUAL ANALYSIS OF "A PORTRAIT OF THE ARTIST AS A YOUNG MAN"

CHAPTER ONE

THE OPENING FUGUE. The first two pages of *A Portrait* are a microcosm of the entire novel. The opening four words suggest that the fairy tale told to Stephen by his father about a cow who came down the road has great symbolic importance; for, later, the priests, more fathers, will promulgate an even greater fairy tale, Irish Catholicism, which Joyce once called "black magic." Stephen must walk down many roads before he finds fulfillment as an incipient artist; he prepares for his European sojourn at the end of the book, determined to follow an even more difficult route. Often he is cuckolded or betrayed, and the name given to him in the fairy tale is appropriate.

Even as a small child, however, Stephen manifests some artistic determination and abilities. His attempt to sing the lines from "Lily Dale" records the lad's confusion through Joyce's splendid use of point-of-view technique. It also anticipates Stephen's later conjecture concerning whether one might actually find a green rose in some distant part of the world. Possibly this imagined place became Paris or Trieste, where Joyce created his own green rose through his writing.

In addition, as the very young boy who will become an artist, Stephen learns to differentiate, an ability put to the test in his elucidation of abstruse Aquinian and Aristotelian precepts in Chapter Five: he perceives that a wet bed feels warm to him at first but that it soon becomes cold. And, again, Stephen notices that his mother has a more pleasant odor than his father, possibly because Simon Dedalus was frequently drunk—as might have been suggested previously by the word "glass," which refers certanly to a monocle but perhaps to a container of stout as well.

Stephen's later difficulties in love and religion are foreshadowed by Dante's insistence that he not play with Eileen Vance, a Protestant. His tutor's fanatical prohibitions are coupled with his mother's indifference to (or ignorance of) the harm being done to his psyche. Mrs. Dedalus reassures her that Stephen will apologize. Dante's reference to the avenging eagles connotes both the fate of Prometheus, doomed to have his intestines picked by a vulture for all eternity, and the fable of Daedalus, the flying, hawklike man. Apparently one must beware of eagles if one is to fly beyond society's restraints. The threat of being blinded, besides suggesting castration in Freudian terms, begins a dominant motif in the novel. Stephen has weak eyes but seemingly more insight than his contemporaries.

OTHER PRELIMINARIES: FATHER FIGURES. At Clongowes, Stephen must find his way through a labyrinth of false fathers (and older "brothers"); of games both in class and out of class, which resemble wars more than mildly competitive academic and physical exercises; and of riddles which he cannot solve. The controlling image of his sojourn at Clongowes is dislocation; but, in his loneliness, Stephen further hones his artistic sensibilities.

The entire book records Stephen's efforts to answer Nasty Roche's question concerning what his father is. Symbolically, is Stephen's father Daedalus, who flew away from the everyday world, or Simon, the extrovert, a man well-grounded in the humdrum and the common? Stephen does not rest secure in his tentative answer, dedication to the Greek Daedalus, in either *A Portrait* or *Ulysses;* and Joyce in the latter chooses for his protagonist Leopold Bloom, the banal advertising canvasser. In *Finnegans Wake,* H.C. Earwicker is certainly of the people, and Joyce turns Stephen into Shem, who is at times a parody of the artist as hero.

THE WAR OF THE ROSES. Stephen's struggle for survival at Clongowes is objectified in the game played during Father Arnall's mathematics lesson. And the game is important for two other reasons: first, the history taught to the boys in this fashionable school is England's, not Ireland's, with the Irish past consigned to legends by the authorities; secondly, Father Arnall does not distinguish between the houses of Lancaster and York, even though the latter was more sympathetic to Irish interests. Stephen's side is the true one, with the House of York represented by the white rose.

RIDDLES. Since Stephen is to be an artist, Joyce shows him wrestling with linguistic puzzles in the early days at school. He cannot answer Wells' enigma when asked if he kisses his mother before he goes to bed, and Wells further humiliates Stephen by adding the words "every night" to his second response. Again, he finds no humor in Brother Michael's insipid retort to the question, "What's up," and later makes no effort to solve Athy's riddle concerning his name. It is tempting to contrast with Stephen's bewilderment Joyce's secure use of the pun in *Finnegans Wake*, which he defended on the basis that the Christian religion is founded upon a play on words: "Thou art Peter, and upon this rock I shall build my church."

ARTISTIC SENSIBILITY. Although Stephen's sensitivity clashes with the coarseness of Clongowes, his artistic sensibilities are not completely frustrated. He begins to find a separate peace for himself. Stephen notices the light music of the gas jets, and it becomes a song for him. He opens and closes the flaps of his ears to drown out the noise of the refectory, and the cessation of sounds reminds him of a train entering a tunnel. Later, he associates the train's entering and leaving with the alternating periods of school and vacation. Again, Stephen tries to define the suggestiveness of words such as suck, cock, and queer, a task necessary for a boy who will some day be a writer as well as for a lad starting to become aware of slightly furtive terms. And he is not content merely to learn spelling from Doctor Cornwell's Spelling Book; for him the euphonious sentences resemble poetry.

SEPARATION AND CLARIFICATION. Analysis is a major ingredient in artistic creation, and at Clongowes Stephen learns to separate, to categorize. Later (after the book ends, in fact), Stephen may acquire the more intuitive ability to synthesize. At Clongowes, however, Stephen breaks things up—partly, in order to be able to cope better with the fragments.

Thus Stephen notices that each boy has a different way of walking, a unique voice, and individually distinctive clothing. All the children have different parents, as well, just as Eileen Vance does. Stephen finds this multitudinousness bewildering and longs to return to his mother or to bed. Nor can he understand how Fleming has colored a page in the geography book green and maroon, the colors of Dante's brushes. Names of states in America and countries in the world at large baffle him.

Some of this bewilderment lightly foreshadows Stephen's later perplexities concerning religion. Stephen wonders why Michael is a brother, not a priest. Is he not holy enough? And he contrasts the holy smell in the nearly empty school's chapel with the distasteful odor of the chapel at Sunday Mass, when peasants attend. Later, at age sixteen, Stephen prays for humility to rectify a major vice: his disdainful attitude towards common people.

THE CHRISTMAS DINNER SCENE: OVERALL VIEW. The Christmas Dinner Scene is one of the most moving individual pieces of writing that Joyce ever composed. In it the destruction of Parnell is delineated through realistically etched characters and dialogue which is so true-to-life that it disguises Joyce's (partly) polemical intention. Autobiographically, Joyce was deeply affected by Parnell's betrayal, and in 1891 he wrote a short piece, "Et Tu, Healy!", which does not survive.

The dinner is the true beginning of Stephen's apostasy, as the young lad wonders how people whom he knows and loves as Catholics can be so divided on the question of their Church's attitude towards Charles Stewart Parnell. A more flexible theological system—if, indeed, there be any—could harbor such dissent, but the rigidity of Irish Catholic dogma condemns divergent thinkers such as Mr. Casey and Simon Dedalus.

CHRISTMAS SYMBOLISM. Significantly, the Christmas dinner is Stephen's first; and, being the eldest child in the family, he is permitted to sit at the table with the adults as the younger children are relegated to the nursery. The Christmas symbolism used here is similar to that employed by Joyce in "The Dead." Christmas is both a season of joy and a time of sorrow: joy because Christ is born, sorrow because He has come into the world to die for man. Christmas occurs in the winter but augurs the rebirth of spring. Here the Christmas dinner anticipates Stephen's later death to an old way of orthodox thinking and foreshadows his resurrection into a life of beginning freedom. The argument sows the seeds for his later break with the Church.

Stephen's future belief that he must fly away from the restraining nets of society is foreshadowed by a seemingly incidental gesture made by Mr. Casey, which captures the emotional moment as well. Impelled by his anger with Dante, Casey leans across the table towards her, "scraping the air from before his eyes with one hand as though he were tearing aside a cobweb."

MOTIFS. The episode is essentially related to Stephen's development in the novel. The turkey reminds him that Mr. Barrett calls his pandybat by that name. He associates the allusion to Parnell's Protestantism with Dante's injunction not to play with Eileen. Stephen hears that Parnell has been hounded like "rats in a sewer," and the phrase blends with the previous picture of his own situation at Clongowes.

Twice the heated language of the debate anticipates future events in Stephen's life. Dante avers that he will remember the anticlerical words of Mr. Casey and Mr. Dedalus when he grows up; in fact, they do eventually drive a wedge between his self-awareness and the totalitarian strictures of the Catholic Church. Again, in his anecdote concerning the harridan who shouted imprecations against Kitty O'Shea, Mr. Casey relates that he called her a name with which he would not sully the ears of the listeners at the dinner table by repeating. Stephen absorbs the comment, wondering what the term could be. He is to find out by the end of Chapter Two, when he begins to frequent prostitutes.

The culmination of Mr. Casey's tale occurs when he relates how he spit into the eye of the old anti-Parnellite. Her response combines two major motifs of the chapter: *"I'm blinded! I'm blinded and drownded!"* Now, the little Stephen can understand only that spitting in the woman's eye was wrong and can relate the event only vaguely to the term which the foulmouthed woman had applied to Parnell's mistress. Later, as Stephen walks towards his partial Baptism by the bird-girl at the end of Chapter Four, he remembers the words, "O, cripes, I'm drownded," and the reader sees their relation to both the Christmas Dinner Scene and Stephen's drenching by Wells at Clongowes. Finally, the adjective, "blinded," suggests Stephen's condition throughout much of the early sections of the novel.

NATURALISM: COMMUNION AND COMMUNICATION. The abstruse symbolism of the Christmas Dinner Scene is realized through realistic details, which contrast the delicious meal with the fact that it is never finished. Some critics see almost every repast in Joyce's works as an analogue of the Eucharistic sacrifice, the Mass. The Christmas Dinner Scene, however, exists in its own right as a powerful and well-integrated passage of Naturalistic writing, whether one wishes to interpret the characters' inability to "communicate" as metaphoric or not.

The Dedalus family was financially secure in Bray, where the scene takes place, and all wait eagerly for the servants to enter. The waste of the bountiful meal becomes even more pathetic since it is one of the last times that the family will enjoy such prosperity. In later chapters Stephen is pictured trying to find sustenance in greasy leftovers, while his starving siblings sing Thomas Moore's *Irish Melodies* in a freezing house. Halfway through the episode, however, Simon realizes the inevitable and can see the violent conclusion that the debate over Parnell will come to.

No amount of preparation or entreaty can stop the bitter quarrel. The careful seating arrangement fails to prevent the participants from shouting and reaching over the table. Mrs. Dedalus' pleas come to naught, and Uncle Charles' senile temporizing fails to stop the flow of words.

The inevitability of the skirmish prevents what could have become mere melodrama in the hands of a lesser writer than Joyce, who skillfully implies that each character is acting out a preconditioned response. Mr. Casey speaks as he must, as does Dante, and once the initial thrusts are made, the scene must be followed to its conclusion. Mrs. Riordan, for example, cannot ignore the anticlerical remarks, and it is inevitable that Mr. Casey, the Fenian, will defend his hatred of the clergy by unfolding the scroll of Irish history—for the clerical administrators were never friends to the Irish nationalists.

Joyce is the master of language in the Christmas Dinner Scene, not a tyrant over it, as some critics claim he is in parts of *Finnegans Wake*. He employs great economy of language in the scene, portraying in a few pages the constant turmoil of "political" Irish families: past, present, and future. The first word of the zealot Dante is a laconic "no," as she covers her plate with her hands. She then objects to Parnell's *public* sins. Mr. Dedalus counters by referring to the pope's nose part of the turkey, and the scene builds in an intricate and plausibly orchestrated way to the controlled conclusion. Here Joyce avoids melodrama again, for Simon's tears, like those of Tennyson in "Tears, Idle Tears," do not fall.

Stephen is to inherit the legacy of doubt enunciated in the episode as Mr. Casey histrionically declaims his preference of atheism over clerical apathy: overlooking the scene, to Stephen's right, is the portrait of the boy's great grandfather.

LATIN LESSON: CLERICAL INJUSTICE. Stephen's unfair treatment by Father Arnall and Father Dolan after his glasses have been smashed is one more beginning step in his ultimate break with the Church. Father Arnall, who passively allows the prefect of studies to punish Stephen, will later perpetrate an even greater injustice upon the boy during the retreat in Chapter Three. Here at Clongowes, however, Stephen begins to doubt the rectitude of clerical judgment. The incident, though, is temporarily forgotten as Stephen succumbs to the ministration of Father Conmee, who seems to have some insight into the lad's problem (and who also may wish to prevent any possible difficulty with Stephen's family).

Unfairness dominates the episode. Stephen reasons that he is the victim of anger generated by the smugging incident—although he cannot yet conceive of homosexuality and attributes his classmates' disgrace to pilfering of altar wine. He shares the sense of communal guilt which the crime arouses, but he is still reluctant to accept punishment for the actions of others.

Arnall treats the class unfairly from the beginning. He insists that all of the themes are to be written over; and he forces Fleming to kneel in the middle of the class, not for failing to answer a question, which the rest of the class missed as well (his ostensible reason), but probably because the pages of Fleming's theme were stuck together by a blot. To save face in front of the school disciplinarian, Arnall lies, averring that Fleming missed all the questions in grammar: he had been asked only one. His other excuse is equally spurious: it is true that Fleming wrote a poor Latin essay, but Arnall has just told the class that all the themes were unacceptable.

The greatest injustice is wreaked upon Stephen, who is entirely innocent of any wrongdoing; and Stephen is much more ingenuous than Fleming, who prepares for clerical wrath by rubbing rosin into his palms. Arnall does not prevent the vicious beating by Dolan, making no attempt to explain that Stephen is justified. He plays the part of Pilate, stating that Stephen is innocent and then standing back while Dolan uses the pandybat. No mention is made of Arnall during the punishment, and Joyce is hinting at the stringency of the clerical hierarchy, with Arnall unwilling to countermand the implied wishes of the prefect of studies.

Dolan is unjust, again, in lifting his pandybat over his shoulder to gain leverage before striking, a practice tacitly forbidden at Clongowes. The smugging affair must indeed have bothered the clerical community! By this pandying episode and by the frequent allusions to the punishment about to be ministered to Big Corrigan, *Joyce is probably commenting upon sexual repressiveness as well as upon academic discipline.*

Father Arnall further demonstrates his hand-washing nature by yoking Stephen and Fleming as common "criminals." Without distinguishing between them, he sends both back to their seats. His soothing voice fails to mitigate the harm he has done, and Stephen muses upon the arbitrariness.

SYMBOLISM: VARIOUS TYPES OF BLINDNESS. The scene fits securely into the symbolic structure of *A Portrait*. It concerns a Latin lesson, the language suggesting that the Catholic Church as a whole is as unfair as the two unjust priests: one acquiesces in doctrines based upon fear; the other actively sponsors them. The blot on Fleming's papers and the awesome sound of Dolan's pandybat striking a desk objectify *Joyce's feelings that Catholicism is grounded in terror and confusion.* The Retreat Sermon, of course, elaborates upon this judgment.

Stephen, who cannot physically see very well, seems to have more insight than his oppressors, and Joyce plays upon the blindness theme in the passage. As Stephen clamors into the center of his class, he is "blinded by fear and haste." Again, Stephen objects to his treatment partially because he is the leader of the Yorkists, the true Irish side. As was seen in the Christmas Dinner episode, however, the Irish clergy was rarely sympathetic to patriots.

The description of Dolan during the pandying is part of the false father theme, with the picture of the prefect's physiognomy filling in the image of Stephen's father at the opening of *A Portrait*. Dolan's quick belief in Stephen's trickery is a projection of his own deceitful nature. As Stephen later discovers through an incidental comment by his father, the pandying and even Father Conmee's ameliorating gestures were simply tactics exercised upon Stephen by Jesuit casuists.

REALISM. Again, Joyce's preachment is anchored in a firm basis of realistic detail. He splendidly captures Stephen's point-of-view during the actual pandying, as Stephen feels sorry for his battered hand; and his picture of the humiliated lad now returned to his seat captures with controlling irony Stephen's continuing inability to "see" —despite the punishment: Stephen hurriedly opens a book, bending over it with his face held near the writing.

REBELLION: MEETING WITH CONMEE. Dolan's pandying and Stephen's protest to Father Conmee take place during Lent and reflect Stephen's death to an old life, religious subservience, and his birth into a new life, his beginning definition of himself as an individual. The clergy had not anticipated Stephen's artistic sensibilities; Stephen recreates the past imaginatively by applying afresh to his own life Richmal Magnall's Questions and the Tales of Peter Parley.

STEPHEN'S CONCEPT OF HIS HERITAGE. Stephen's decision to visit Father Conmee springs, symbolically, from his sense of heritage with the Greek Daedalus. Joyce calls attention to Stephen's last name by having the boy wonder why Father Dolan could not remember it when he was told the first time. Was the prefect inattentive, or did he wish to ridicule the name? Stephen's classmates urge him in the name of the Roman Senate to rectify Dolan's injustice; and, even though their entreaties stem from a desire to identify vicariously with the young rebel while he takes all the chances, Stephen does not care to examine their motives. On the way to Conmee's office Stephen sees the portraits of Ignatius Loyola and Francis Xavier staring down at him, even as the portrait of his great grandfather had shadowed the Christmas Dinner Scene. And, with his imagination stimulated further, he again recreates the legend of the patriot, Hamilton Rowan.

The meeting with Father Conmee helps restore some of Stephen's equilibrium. His fear when approaching the rector is increased by the self-doubt inculcated by Father Dolan, who told him that he had the look of a schemer. Stephen had even wanted a mirror to check out the prefect's judgment. Conmee, however, does help Stephen—even if his motives are mixed.

STEPHEN'S MOTIVATIONS. Stephen's reasons for confronting Conmee are clearly delineated and include more than the protagonist's wish to live up to his heritage. He believes Dolan's threat that he will visit the class the next day and knows that he may be punished again. Stephen fears that he is entering a labyrinth of anger, since the smugging affair still occupies the emotions of the clergy. He is afraid, too, that he may fail in his appeal to Conmee and thus draw further wrath from the disciplinarian's seemingly endless store. In addition, he is afraid of the jeers of his schoolmates should Conmee turn against him. Yet, Stephen feels that he has been deceitfully used and proceeds on his trip. Corrigan deserved punishment, he realizes, but he does not.

Joyce again chooses his details carefully. Stephen knows that he is being observed by his colleagues as he enters the corridor leading to Conmee's room; and the appointments of the rector's stuffy office, including a prominently displayed skull, do little to reassure the frightened lad.

CONMEE'S SUBTLETY. Father Conmee's subtlety is a contrast to the boorishness of Father Dolan and the ineffectuality of Father Arnall. Although Conmee's sympathy with Stephen may come in part from a desire to avoid a complaint from the family, Conmee does emerge as one of the better people in *A Portrait*. Still, his ways are those of the skillful administrator and Jesuit casuist, and one must weigh the importance of Stephen's revelation that he has informed his parents of the broken glasses.

Conmee succeeds in exonerating both sides, Stephen's and Dolan's. When Stephen answers definitively that Dolan was indeed apprised of the situation, Conmee must find another route to avoid contradicting the school disciplinarian. Stephen avers that he was pandied after he had informed Father Dolan of the broken glasses; but Conmee quickly asks whether Stephen told Dolan that he had written for replacements. Stephen is forced to answer "no" and to accept Conmee's judgment that the whole affair was a mistake. In much the same way Stephen cannot see through the artifice of the Retreat Sermon at the time but does see its falsity upon further reflection.

SUCCESS AND WITHDRAWAL. Stephen, for his part, has succeeded as well. He has averted the specter of Dolan's threat and lived up to his father's counsel never to peach on a fellow. In several ways Stephen has been faithful to his legacy, notwithstanding the fact that he later learns that the whole affair was treated as a joke by the clergymen involved.

Unable to succeed in athletics, to be led from the field by devoted followers of sports, Stephen does succeed as a rebel and is accepted by the group. His destiny, however, is to be always alone, and the chapter concludes with his breaking free from admiring schoolmates. At the end of the section, Joyce sets Stephen apart from his friends, who have won their vicarious victory. They carry him along for a time, but Stephen successfully struggles against the confining bonds of their acceptance. *The true artist must escape all entanglements,* approbation as well as censure, and Stephen is alone as the other boys give three cheers for Conmee and three groans for Dolan. Stephen is determined to tread his way unassisted through the labyrinth of life.

CHAPTER TWO

BEAUTY AND DECAY: BLACKROCK. The opening pages of this chapter describe Stephen's failing attempts to escape from the harsh, "realistic" facts of human life. Stephen is continually pulled down to earth by the sordidness of his environment. Some critics have not been impressed by the protagonist's Byronic efforts to rise above the encumbering clay, however, seeing a cloacal obsession on the part of Joyce at the root of the naturalistic detail in the section.

The opening of the chapter, with Uncle Charles sitting in the out-house, contrasts with the ending of Chapter One, where Stephen is exalted by his classmates: it is now accepted by most critics that Joyce employs a technique of "inflation" followed by "deflation" in the novel. For example, Chapter Four ends with Stephen's vision of his Pagan Mary, and Chapter Five begins in the meager surroundings of the Dedalus household, with Simon asking Stephen's sister whether her "lazy bitch of a brother" has left yet.

MORAL PARALYSIS. Often moments of elevation are commingled with moments of grotesque and depressing detail. Uncle Charles dresses carefully for his morning's defecation, which is helped by the black twist. He sings as he sits, perhaps finding the lyrics "mollifying." *Joyce may have in mind the Freudian conception of defecation as creativity,* as he assuredly does in the Calypso Episode of *Ulysses,* when Bloom sits and thinks of writing for *Titbits.* The concept is applied ironically, of course, to Stephen's attenuated granduncle.

Joyce places Uncle Charles and Mike Flynn on the stage at the start of the chapter to suggest some of the difficulties Stephen will encounter on his journey towards seraphic creation. He uses a similar technique in "The Sisters," the opening story of *Dubliners.* Here the paralyzed priest, who has died before the story begins, objectifies the theme of the collection of short stories, the moral paralysis of Ireland. Flynn is a caricature of a human being, a trainer of sprinters who is completely out of shape himself. One is not surprised to learn that Flynn has entered the hospital.

Again, *the pastoral interlude* enjoyed with Aubrey Mills soon ends with the coming of autumn. The milkman's cows are driven away from the grass, and the cowyard becomes an oozing fen. *Stephen is unable to accept life:* he cannot bring himself to consume the cows' milk.

Often the lines are sprinkled with more subtle references to the life which Stephen finds repugnant. Uncle Charles sprinkles holy water on Stephen, and some of it falls onto the floor; he reads the smudged prayerbook above his breath.

The dual motifs of beauty and decay are illustrated by allusions to grapes. Uncle Charles associates grapes with the bowels; to Stephen they help recreate the romantic escapades of the Count of Monte Cristo: Stephen sees himself speaking to Mercedes with mild disdain and refusing the muscatel grapes. In Chapter Five he rejects grapes again when he will not receive Holy Eucharist.

STEPHEN'S HIDDEN VISION. Through all of the barrenness of the Blackrock sojourn, however, Stephen furtively nourishes his idealism. He resembles the pre-adolescent hero of Joyce's "Araby," who finds the litanies of shop boys and cries of juvenile playmates crass after he has fallen in what he thinks is love for the first time. In *A Portrait* Stephen dreams of Mercedes even while he is playing childish games with Aubrey Mills. The dominant image of his search for beauty and escape from family poverty is one which occurs later, after Stephen has fallen into serious sin and feels cut off from the radiance of his vision: the tiny whitewashed house with several rosebushes growing in its garden, which he pretends is the home of a contemporary Mercedes.

Joyce carefully distinguishes Stephen's meanderings in the imagination from those of his playmates. Stephen desires to meet in its actualized form the disembodied figment of his soul's imaginings. Stephen realizes that he will never find his dream by seeking it in specific ways. It will encounter him and will transform him, much as Christ was transfigured before his ascent into Heaven. Ironically, at the end of the chapter his vision does encounter him—as a prostitute pulls the reluctant lad towards her. The temporary security which she affords him is quickly lost by the machinations of another prostitute, the Whore of Babylon, during the retreat.

DUBLIN: ECONOMIC DISLOCATION. The family's economic instability further isolates Stephen from his dream. The vans which move the family from Blackrock are yellow, as is the scum which lies on the Liffey River. Stephen's mother weeps as the family travels to its new home, and her tears recall her reaction in Chapter One to

Stephen's departure to Clongowes. Then she wore a veil to cover her emotions, and Stephen pretended not to notice that she was about to cry. Here, in Dublin, and at Blackrock Stephen shares the family's grief, his guilt perhaps augmented by his being the oldest in the family.

Joyce's details contribute to a picture of Stephen's loneliness. In the new home the fires will not light, and the table lamp casts a tepid glow on the bare floors, which have been dirtied by the shoes of the movers. Stephen's father recites his troubles in a disjointed monologue. Dublin's fog mirrors an emotional miasma. And Stephen is saddened by thoughts of the depressingly stark new home. Even the policemen who patrol the Dublin quays are dishevelled.

STEPHEN'S RENEWED GESTATION. Through all the degradation, however, a new and better Stephen begins to emerge, as Joyce seems to suggest a concept later developed by Edmund Wilson in his "Wound and the Bow" theory of artistic creation: often creativity depends upon the catalyst of psychic and emotional pain—and Dublin does give Stephen a large dose of personal freedom. No longer are his peripatetic wanderings hampered by Uncle Charles, who has grown too senile to be trusted with the errands. Timid at first, Stephen soon decides to map out the city (as did Joyce) and to examine its corners. At the end of the chapter one of these lanes leads to his assignation with the prostitute.

Stephen finds Dublin new and "complex," the latter a key term for describing his precise mental state. Like the protagonist in "An Encounter," Stephen wanders by the wharfs, dreaming of far places and distant music. Already he is preparing for his journey to Europe. His vision of Mercedes has been combined with a wish to visit the actual places mentioned in *The Count of Monte Cristo*.

FOUR VIGNETTES. Four pictures of Stephen's life in Dublin present aspects of his growing personality. In the first his maternal aunt is interrupted in her contemplation of a newspaper photograph of the lovely Mabel Hunter, who is appearing in a Dublin pantomime, probably one presented at the Gaiety Theatre. Stephen finds that the enchantment of the moment is broken by a clumsy boy carrying coals into the room. The lad dispatches his load onto the floor and fumbles at the paper with his coarse fingers. In a second sketch Stephen is mistaken by Ellen for Josephine and is seemingly embarrassed by the girl's laughter, which peals out following the mistake. At this time Stephen is having problems of sexual identity, and the episode lightly points to these implied difficulties.

The other two pictures are more significant. During a party at Harold's Cross, Stephen experiences two emotions concerning the mass of people, which conflicting feelings are to plague him throughout the novel: a restraint and aloofness when dealing with common pleasures mixed with a wish to be part of the group's simple enjoyments. He soon grows weary of the games played by the children and perhaps fears that his somber appearance might dampen their merry spirits. He tries to savor his isolation but quickly finds that the amusements might indeed serve a more useful function: the involvement of the others in their pastimes prevents them from detecting the hidden feelings that are surging deep within him. These emotions are stimulated by the glance of an interested girl, and he is found out in spite of himself.

This picture differs considerably from the former image of Stephen as he nurses a private grief over the family's ruined finances. At least, now, he can relate to someone outside of himself; he is becoming less solipsistic.

In the last of the four vignettes, Stephen refuses to kiss a young girl, Emma, and the delicacy of his tentative advances and subsequent withdrawal contrasts sharply with his lewd involvement with the prostitute at the chapter's end. It is significant that on the last tram (Stephen's farewell to Pre-Lapsarian sexlessness?) Emma makes the approach. In *Ulysses* we are told what Stephen really thought about on street cars—naked women!—but here Joyce portrays his protagonist as the evader of traps, the Daedalus.

As in "The Dead," the emotional separation of the flirting "lovers" is symbolized by physical distance. Just as

Gabriel Conroy helplessly watched his wife, Gretta, who was at the top of the stairs, probably thinking of her lost love, Michael Furey, so Stephen is separated from his friend by the structure of the two-storied tram. He thinks that she wants him to hold her, that this is her reason for ascending the steps so many times.

What Stephen fears most of all in the fourth vignette is rejection, being laughed at as he was when mistaken for Josephine or when he and Eileen watched waiters secure decorations on the flagstaff. Then Eileen's reaction had been sudden. Now Stephen opposes to his incipient physiological urges not the later weapons of "silence, exile, and cunning," but a more dangerous withdrawal and tranquility. As he tears his ticket to bits, however, Stephen realizes that a more effective way must be found to deal with problems much greater than grim finances.

TOUCH OF THE POET: EMMA CLERY. Stephen's first efforts at poetry are important not for their literary forms but for the picture they provide of a young man who has yet to master the art of the concrete, the common. Already Stephen is formulating the process by which the artist refines himself "out of existence," the final stage in his later schema of artistic distance. In Chapter Two, however, objectivity is gained only by sacrificing the real. Somewhat in the manner of much Decadent writing, "phenomena" are lost in the search for "noumena." Not until he created Leopold Bloom, the man of facts, did Joyce fully succeed in translating Epiphanic moments into actualities.

The poetry that Stephen writes to Emma Clery, in the manner of Lord Byron, is in part wish-fulfillment. In his reveries he is able to bestow upon Emma the kiss withheld from her on the tram; and both young people are united in the type of Heaven suggested in the poetry of the Celtic school and in the very early writings of Yeats.

The poem begun to E.C. is the work of a young man who still commingles religion and art without being aware of their contradictory premises. He is soon to discover, in his confrontation with Heron and Heron's two cohorts, that choosing Byron over Tennyson can be costly. Later still,

Stephen will follow the path of self-exile that Byron chose almost a century before.

It is significant that the Byronic title of Stephen's poem is the first item to appear on the page after another set of initials, A.M.D.G., the Jesuit motto, "Ad Majorem Dei Gloriam," i.e., "to the greater glory of God." Joyce might well be suggesting that the artistic life in Stephen's case will indeed afford God "greater glory." The first incursion into the pain of the creative process ends with another religious motto, L.D.S., "Laus Deo Semper," i.e., "praise to God always." *Stephen's balancing of sex, art, and religion is tenuous, and the equilibrium is perforce transitory.*

The nets through which Stephen must break are woven of nationalism as well as religion. Stephen writes his poetry in an emerald exercise book, probably one issued to commemorate the approaching centennial of the 1798 Rising, and he is distracted from his composition by thoughts of the argument over Parnell during the Christmas Dinner scene. As a child he had tried to write a poem about Parnell's martyrdom; but now, as a growing artist, Stephen is beginning to realize that the true poet is beyond partisan politics. Stephen manifests this doctrine in Chapter Five by refusing to sign MacCann's peace petition and to protest against Yeats' *The Countess Cathleen.*

REALISTIC VIEW OF CLONGOWES. This episode places into perspective Stephen's heroic complaint to Father Conmee concerning his unfair treatment by Father Dolan. Joyce does not describe Stephen's reactions to his father's recital of his meeting with the former principal of Clongowes but allows the section to end on a note of laughter as the priests reduce Stephen's fears (and courage) to a joke: the laugh is on Stephen. The poignancy of such a revelation need not be spelled out, and here Joyce allows the event to speak for itself. The clerical actions are one more reason for Stephen's eventual break with the Church.

The episode shows once again Joyce's skilled use of sources. "Conmee" was not made provincial until 1906; Joyce steps up the process: a shallow (but, in some ways, commiserate) casuist is rewarded before he deserves the elevation.

Joyce stresses both the crassness of Stephen's father and his sycophantic relation to even more fawning priests. His point depends upon the reader's recollection of Stephen's treatment by Dolan and explains why so much time was spent detailing Stephen's physical pain and emotional anguish in the episode.

The setting for Stephen's rejection is, once again, a meal which is not enjoyed and reminds one of the uneaten food of the Christmas Dinner scene. Again, Stephen is destined not to communicate; instead, he becomes the devoured sheep of the mutton hash.

Simon appreciates the worldly nature of the Jesuits, and his reference to their overflowing dinner tables reflects Joyce's recurrent theme of *simony, the buying and selling of sacred things.* Mr. Dedalus is gratified that his son will be attending Belvedere, a Jesuit school, that he will be able to avoid the Christian Brothers, who do not understand the ways of the world as well as members of the Society of Jesus. Autobiographically, Joyce did attend the Christian Brothers school for a time. Stephen, however, studies only with the superficially successful Jesuits, and his final break with the Church becomes all the more convincing.

Joyce wants the reader to see this seemingly unimportant episode as one large step in Stephen's emotional growth. He explicitly relates the scene to the Christmas Dinner fiasco by having Mr. Dedalus push his plate towards Stephen. Mr. Casey had performed a similar gesture before telling how he repaid the old harridan who called Kitty O'Shea the foul name. In the present episode, of course, Simon's gesture suggests, in addition, that he is urging his son to swallow much more than food.

THE WHITSUNTIDE PLAY. Stephen's part as "farcical pedagogue" in the evening performance foreshadows the role of ironic prophet that he will play in Chapter Five, when he preaches his gospel of art to reluctant classmates. In Chapter Two the theatre in which the play is staged becomes for Stephen an amphitheatre of the mind wherein the conflict between idealism and reality is first codified in *A Portrait*. Joyce intends a symbolic theatre; he himself acted in a play called *Vice Versa*, which burlesques the antagonism betwen father and son. As he was to do in *Finnegans Wake*, Joyce uses here farcical elements to delineate a serious theme. Also, the episode is related to the trip to Cork; there Stephen's realization that other teenagers (besides himself) have sexual fantasies occurs in an anatomy theatre.

In this theatre of life Stephen begins to discover his personality and, in addition, to formulate an aesthetic theory. He learns that he is no longer moved by platitudinous statements about honor, nationalism, and the value of a vigorous physical life. Now he senses that he differs from the others who worship such abstractions; in *Ulysses* Stephen tells Mr. Deasy, in "Nestor," that he abhors the big words which make us so unhappy.

Stephen's dawning sense of artistic unity is seen in his perception of the suddenness by which all the elements of his play coalesce. Later, he was to call this *Gestalt* "claritas," a vision of the radiance which issues from a harmoniously constructed and complete object or idea.

Joyce takes great pains to set the stage for Stephen's beginning replacement of religious ideals with secular ones. The Blessed Sacrament has been removed from the tabernacle to make room for the evening's merriment, and the theatre itself is described as an ark several times in the chapter: the allusion both suggests the motley nature of the performances and also implies that Stephen may find a new world of the spirit after his vessel has landed on dry land. The Whitsuntide or Pentecost setting suggests that the tongues of flames will bring Stephen power to speak in various languages—not as a preacher, but as a writer whose purpose is to forge anew the conscience of his benighted Irish race.

Stephen's new consciousness is seen first in his rejection of the type of honor which the superficial Heron insists upon. When the angry Mr. Boyle inquires after Stephen, Heron counsels Stephen to disdain the command; and this false bravado reminds Stephen of the commands of his father and of his Clongowes and Belvedere teachers. He is tired of being a "gentleman" above all else—although he respects Cardinal Newman's writings. At Clongowes he carried out his father's injunction not to peach on a fellow student during the meeting with Conmee, only to learn that he was patronized and laughed at behind his back.

Stephen rejects, also, the precepts of manliness advocated by Irish nationalists, and his refusal to conform to the demands of the Gaelic League (founded in 1893) foreshadows his later decision not to study Gaelic. These demands, coupled with the responsibilities of being the oldest child in a starving family, all seem to him hollow sounding and unromantic.

One obsession, however, Stephen cannot break free from, his vaguely understood attachment to Emma—now or by the end of *A Portrait*. Just as the narrator of "Araby" is chagrined by the common sounds of the streets as he carries his chalice of love through a "throng of foes," so Stephen is annoyed by his friends' crass insinuations about his relationship with Emma. He nurses his dreams about her in secret, remembering how he failed to kiss her on the streetcar. Unable to understand the emotional tumult which she has occasioned, he looks forward to her presence at the play.

When all of the faces are familiar at the conclusion of Stephen's play, he realizes that he has fallen prey to his feelings. This episode parallels Stephen's refusal to speak to Emma in Chapter Five because of his conviction that she has been flirting with a priest. Now, however, he finds a more pungent solution to his romantic problems, inhaling the odor of horse's urine in order to obviate the troubles of adolescent love.

Joyce does suggest, however, that Stephen may some day be able to balance the conflicting imperatives of sexual love and artistic creation. A few moments before Stephen's performance, the garb of aloofness is stripped away from his boyishness as Emma's "serious alluring eyes" act as catalyst to his youthful passions. In a matter of seconds, though, he is thoroughly involved in his part, the whole coming together in an almost preternatural manner. *Perhaps Joyce is describing the mild schizophrenia common to many writers.*

Set against Stephen's struggles to find himself is the sterile complacency of the clergy and lay prefects, whose mincing gestures and fawning acquiesence in the established order reflect Joyce's view that Ireland is indeed sterile. And Joyce accompanies this picture of obsequiousness with veiled references to the sexual inadequacies of the priests and masters. In Chapter Four the Director knowingly warns Stephen away from the Capuchins: their skirts are too full.

Mr. Tate typifies the sorry leader that Stephen is meant to emulate. Joyce presents Tate's limitations, both social and sexual, with excellent compression during the scene in which Stephen is accused, half-facetiously, of heresy. Joyce calls attention to his hand delving between his thighs and to the starched shirt, which serves to shackle the English master. Stephen thinks of his own worn collar as the mock Inquisitor denounces him to the group. Stephen's collar indicates his imprisonment in two types of squalor: the filth (as he sees it) of his mind and the physical sordidness of his home. Stephen, however, manages to escape from his confining garb; Tate does not.

The actions of other prefects and priests are equally sleazy and perhaps even more suggestive. One priest smiles beneath the glow of a lantern; and another flaps his soutane at a group of tardy children. A third delights in Bertie Tallon's female attire, and Stephen feels annoyed at the merriment gained at the boy's obvious discomfiture. The other boys admire the makeup, duped perhaps by the clerical approbation.

HERON: A BIRD-LIKE ENEMY.   Joyce's physical description of Heron is that of a bird, presumably the type of creature that might challenge a human aviator such as Stephen's Greek namesake. Heron's croaking voice resembles a bird's as do his shock of hair, his bony forehead, and his beaked nose. In the flashback to the episode following Tate's accusation, Heron seems to be part of a flock of predators which attacks Stephen: he is accompanied by his cohort, Nash, who approaches Stephen "wagging his great red head."

Heron is Stephen's rival, just as Buck Mulligan is in *Ulysses*. He is intelligent but superficial, a rival (as Joyce stresses), but an opponent who lacks Stephen's depth and potential. In *Ulysses* Stephen must steer a narrow course between rigid Dublin Catholicism and the seductive blasphemy of Oliver Gogarty—and Heron shares much of the latter's propensity for the profane.

Joyce carefully compares the intelligence of the two schoolboys, referring to their dual leadership of a cloddish Belvedere class, and then carefully distinguishing between them. Stephen at this point of *A Portrait* is not as out-wardly secure as the cynical and self-possessed Hern is more willing to see blemishes in himself and to rectify them in a way that will not c ideals.

Heron's reference to Emma desecrates St of his loved one as a cross between the M. Cathleen ni Houlihan. The "soft peal of mirthles which the sinister youngster lets escape from relates him to the goatlike creatures, *symbols of lu.* which Stephen dreams in Chapter Three: "Soft la issued from their spittleless lips ... "

Objectivity suggests, however, that Stephen's deep tagonism towards Heron stems in part from the he barely conscious feeling that his devotion to Emma mig be mainly a matter of sex. Despite their differences, then Stephen and Heron do share a common physiology, no matter how deftly each tries to hide it by posturing. The judgment that Stephen is not a saint is repeated in *Ulysses*.

The threat which Heron poses to Stephen's symbolic father is objectified in his pointed references to Stephen's physical father, Simon. Heron is a bird who pecks away at Stephen's weak spot. He abruptly introduces the subject of Simon Dedalus into the conversation and disquiets the protagonist. In the flashback Heron and his companions speak of the books owned by their fathers, and Stephen is puzzled by their sudden stress upon learning; Boland and Nash are scarcely stellar pupils. Heron poses a danger because he has discovered blemishes in Stephen which cannot possibly lose their tinct.

TWO REFUSALS TO ADMIT: SUFFERING FOR ART. Heron's insistence that Stephen admit his attachment to Emma reminds Stephen of another time when his rival tried to force a confession from him—and failed. The two incidents are parallel in that both involve Stephen's secret and passionate devotion. It does not really matter that Emma is scarcely worth the defense or that the Byronic mask is in many ways adolescent. More important is that Stephen believes deeply in his ideas and will not have them compromised. Although based in part upon his defensive reaction to a sordid environment, Stephen's refusal to "admit" that Tennyson is a better poet than the notorious Byron foreshadows his later insistence on art for the sake of art.

The attempt by the unholy Trinity of Heron, Boland, and Nash to trap Stephen is analogous to the Pharisaical efforts of Christ's enemies, who insisted that he choose between God and Caesar. Stephen, in fact, does render to God by agreeing that Cardinal Newman (whose title he omits, only to be corrected for his irreverence) is the finest writer of prose; but, about poetry, he will tolerate no compromise. Stephen is "crucified" against a barbed wire fence, and Joyce's description of the lashing administered to him suggests Christ's Scourging at the Pillar. Stephen's defense of a heretic looks forward to his later apostasy.

Again, Stephen is midway through a struggle, not completely secure, and he does partially capitulate to the dictates of his peer group. His "confession" to Heron on the night of the play is made in Latin, the *Confiteor*, as Stephen disguises his fear of complete rejection. In addition, in the flashback, Stephen does recant and explains to Tate that his intention in the essay was orthodox. Later, Heron and his friends chide him for giving in to the master. The mature Joyce, however, like the quickly growing Stephen, refuses to abide by another's judgment in matters of artistic creation.

Finally, it is appropriate that Stephen should be cited for heresy in Tate's class and that his error should deal with the approach to a perfect state. Later, Stephen discovers that perfection is possible not in the Church but only through a mastery of literary form.

TRIP TO CORK. Two powerful forces combine in this episode to lead Stephen to the prostitute at the chapter's conclusion. Stephen's realization that his father and he, despite external appearances, are really quite different persons is coupled with his discovery that impure thoughts and desires are not common only to him. His visit to the prostitute is the inevitable outcome of a sense of loneliness and isolation joined with his explicit perception of sexual need. By the end of the chapter, Stephen has come a long way from his love poems to E.C., which ingenuously blended Byronic romance with religious mottoes.

Joyce uses the image of the moon's apparent similarity with the stars—but its essential difference from them—to contrast the extroverted Simon with his shy son. Joyce probably expects the reader to look up the line from Shelley's "Fragment" that follows the three lines quoted in the section: "Among the stars that have a different birth." Clearly, the line depicts what Stephen feels to be his relationship with his father. The pain of lost security which Stephen experiences in this chapter foreshadows his desolation when cut off from his Heavenly father in the next.

Paternity itself forms a dominant motif in the episode. Simon Dedalus is selling his heritage by committing to auction the last of his properties. Old Johnny Cashman becomes a living symbol of the paternity theme: his memory, inspired by drink, supposedly reaches back four generations.

Stephen can neither accept the mellow sense of the past expressed in his father's drunken sentimentality nor match his present personality and disposition with Simon's ideals of manhood. Stephen is well aware of the somber purpose of the journey to Cork; his father uses the trip to evoke memories of an imagined past, all the time squandering his remaining money on drink.

Burdened by deep guilt and numbing insecurity, Stephen perceives the limitless gap which exists between his father's seeming zest for life and his own social inadequacies. For a time, Simon's singing drives away Stephen's depression, but the clouds quickly return as his father is gulled by the fawning porter on the way to the anatomy theatre.

Stephen is no match for his gregarious father; neither has he yet discovered his own complete individuality. When young, for example, Simon belonged to a group of "gentlemen" all of whom had some specific talent; Stephen, of course, feels that he can do nothing that would interest another. Simon recalls that his father was so handsome that women stopped and stared at him; Stephen feels weak and lonely. Simon's harmless flirtations become traumatically humiliating for Stephen, who projects his own sense of the sordidness of sex onto his father's empty boasting.

So intense is Stephen's isolation from the world of his Micawber-like father that he feels himself fading away and must think explicitly of his name and location in order to locate his personality in the actual. The many past references to death in *A Portrait* now are seen as metaphors of Stephen's psychic state. In Cork, Stephen experiences *the desolation of spirit that precedes renewal,* although in such a condition neither Stephen nor anyone else can usually see the light in the future. Stephen's Everyman journey takes place on a mail train.

FOETUS. It is appropriate that a major illumination should occur in an anatomy theatre. The setting carries through the motif of the play, prominent in the chapter; and Stephen is being dissected, with special attention expended upon his spiritual anatomy. The episode is acted out in darkness, with the Charon-like porter leading Simon to the desk in which he once carved his initials.

Joyce calls special attention to the word *Foetus:* it is typical of what one would expect to find in an anatomy theatre; but, most important, *it foreshadows Stephen's rebirth.* Now he is not fully formed. Joyce's symbolic intent is seen in his description of the wood in which *"Foetus"* is etched: "dark stained."

Stephen finds the images suggested by the medical term both repugnant and compelling. They objectify his own growing awareness of powerful sexual drives, and the vision of past students called forth by the word is more vivid than that summoned up by his father's rambling descriptions. Stephen imagines a rudely dressed, strong young man with a moustache, carefully etching each letter, a youth resembling the physical Lynch of Chapter Five, who puts out his chest as a criticism of life. The lad's classmates joke as he limns "Foetus"; by contrast, Stephen sees in their health and bodily well-being only his own ineptitudes and desecrations. Yet, the episode has catapulted Stephen into a world far removed from the universe of pious ejaculations, vague poems imitative of Decadence writings, and light dilemmas about whether to kiss or not to kiss on empty trams. Judging himself too harshly, Stephen sees all his past heroics as empty posturings; everything is leveled by his obsessive feelings of guilt.

The last pages of Chapter Two, ending with the visit to the prostitute, trace Stephen's final attempts to adhere to an old, ethical code of life, to avoid "sin." The levee of Stephen's personality is overflooded by sexual passions, and Stephen's failure of will reflects one of Joyce's own reasons for leaving the formal practice of Catholicism: he felt that he was unable physiologically to abide by the restrictions.

Nothing works for Stephen: nothing can curb the flow—not the rules which he imposes upon his family to dispose of the funds recently awarded to him; not the trips to the theatre to see *Ingomar* or *The Lady of Lyons;* not the occasional, dim recollections of Mercedes or of the small, whitewashed house on the path leading to the mountains. Only on occasion can Stephen identify with the hero of Bulwer-Lytton's *The Lady of Lyons,* Claude Melnotte, who wins many glories with Napoleon's army and eventually attains the beautiful Pauline Deschappelles. Stephen's life is as unfinished as the wainscot of his bedroom after the money neded to buy more paint runs out.

Stephen is besieged by night as well as by day, with objects and persons harmless in daylight transmogrified into beings of lust and sin in his dreams. The description foreshadows Stephen's vision of the goat-like creatures of Chapter Three and also looks forward to the Circe Episode of *Ulysses*, in which, at midnight, the brothel area of Dublin becomes a nightmare of all types of inversion. On a more mundane level, Stephen's dreams probably lead to nocturnal emissions, which, with his tender conscience, he judges riots of sexual promiscuity.

By day, Stephen still searches for the indefinable objectifications of his longings; now, however, he yearns not for a materialization of his love for Mercedes but for the more realistic relief of tumescence. Overstating his sexual "fall," Stephen sees his early aspirations as no more sanctified than the graffiti on the "oozing" wall of a urinal.

The setting of Stephen's visit to the prostitute has elements of a Black Mass, as Stephen replaces his religious obsession (temporarily) with an abandonment to his sexual, "lower" nature. Yellow again becomes the color of decay, and the gasflames of the prostitutes' hovels burn like candles on an altar. The rites for which little groups come together are those of sex, not religion, although, as is implied throughout *A Portrait*, the dresses of the whores might well resemble the cassocks of priests prepared to assist at the Eucharistic sacrifice.

Stephen battles to the last before surrendering his person to the temporary security of sexual intercourse. He is the one seduced as he is escorted from the "middle" of the street by the prostitute who detains him (the word "detains" suggests the later discussion of this term with the *Dean of Studies*. There, citing linguistic and philological problems, Stephen paraphrases Newman, who wrote that the Virgin Mary was "detained in the full company of the saints"). Again, Stephen stands in the center of the prostitute's lair, and she must come to him. Stephen will not bend to kiss the woman: his refusal connotes both his stalwart resolution to shore up his last ounce of resistance and, more significantly, his desire to be held and absorbed by a reassuring mother figure. At the touch of the prostitute's lips, Stephen abandons himself to a sub-stratum of emotion far different from the teachings of religion or the sublimation of Byronic sexual acrobatics into poetry.

The tawdriness of the prostitute contrasts with Stephen's idealism at the start of the chapter: her pink dress, her obscene doll, her final injunction to Stephen to kiss her. Joyce may well have had in mind the nickname of William Butler Yeats when he has the prostitute address Stephen as Willie. Certainly, Stephen is no longer governing his life by the 1880's poetry of his elder, which deals, in part, with dreamy maidens in ethereal settings. Stephen's focus now is on the real, even though, with his extremist nature, the actual has become the lurid—both physically and spiritually.

CHAPTER THREE

THE DEADLY SINS. Before the Retreat Sermon, Stephen is held in the grip of the Seven Deadly Sins; and Joyce's source for the first few pages of Chapter Three is probably the belief of St. James (an ironic choice of saint!) that a violation of one commandment involves transgressing all the others. Stephen's gluttony is revealed in his new attitude towards food, as the young Momus no longer eats merely to ward off starvation in the impoverished Dedalus household, but wishes to cram his stomach with highly seasoned victuals. Again, he projects his own slothful ways onto the prostitutes, whom he imagines yawning lazily as they arrange their hair. His senses delight in the imagined words of beckoning whores. Mired in sin, Stephen is lost in *accidie,* indifference to his grievous faults, which have become easier to commit after the initial capitulation.

All sins are traceable to pride eventually, and Stephen exhibits this vice in his condescension towards those whom he considers beneath his level of sensitivity. His psyche rankles at Ennis' stammering definition of "surd": in mathematics, an irrational number. He scorns the worshippers who stand lined up outside of church during Mass in the belief that they are fulfilling their Sunday religious obligation. Stephen's pride is not without its heroism, however, and he refuses to pray before bed even though he realizes the Almighty may cast his soul into Hell should he die in sleep. This refusal to placate the Divinity by even a short ejaculation foreshadows his courageous choice in Chapter Five to leave Church and country, to take a chance on being damned eternally for his apostasy.

Stephen's obsession with sex is seen in the transformation of the equation in his scribbler into the heavily Freudian "widening tail," which resembles the "worm" that Mr. Duffy sees at the end of "A Painful Case."

Three motifs delineate Stephen's plight. His "circling always nearer and nearer" as he approaches the brothel district foreshadows his later dream of the goatish creatures, whose circling threatens to enclose him; secondly, Shelley's fragment to the moon serves as contrast to Stephen's present state. No longer are the stars and moon clearly differentiated, but now all is disintegrating before Stephen's eyes. Finally, Stephen's spiritual desolation is seen in terms of literal dryness, with the fountains of sanctifying grace no longer replenishing his soul. The drops of water mentioned at the end of Chapter One cease to fill the cup of his life.

RETREAT SERMON: STEPHEN AS INDIVIDUAL. Added to Stephen's sense of sin when faced with the prospect of a retreat are complications arising from his own specific personality. In the sometimes sentimental manner of Dowson and Verlaine, his attitude towards the Virgin Mary is like Dowson's posture towards Cynara: a desecration of the beloved, accompanied by feelings of guilt and self-pity. Mary is the Refuge of Sinners, and Stephen makes sure that he needs her assistance. In the Nausicaa Episode of *Ulysses*, Joyce parodies the title of Mary, the "morning star," by his picture of the flirtatious, crippled Gerty MacDowell.

Stephen's moral problems are increased by his persistent need for theological pedantics. He succors the poor, for example, in the hope of receiving actual grace, the dynamic, divine thrust which activates the soul towards the stasis of sanctifying grace. Stephen's contradictory needs, his desire both to denigrate the godhead and his residual wish to approach God "nearer," are objectified in his position as sodality prefect. One suspects that he keeps the scroll in full vision partially so that he can brood upon the enormity of his sins.

The brilliance of Joyce's Retreat Sermon lies not merely in his realistic depiction of a dreadful aspect of Catholicism, which has afflicted many believers, but also in Joyce's clear use of point-of-view. Because of the uniqueness of his personality, Stephen suffers inordinately from Arnall's fervid moralizing, while most of his classmates can take in stride the fire and brimstone of the exhortations. The Retreat Sermon is true Naturalism, not because of its lurid details, which, despite protests of some Joyceans to the contrary, do describe abuses still being perpetrated in many Catholic schools, but rather because it operates upon a psyche already molded by a number of individualized, powerful forces. Stephen's preparation for the Retreat Sermon began on the first page of *A Portrait;* and, if any one of the major events in the first two chapters of the novel had been omitted, the effect of the Retreat Sermon would have been weakened. The stage of the sermon is Stephen's mind, and Stephen feels, through Joyce's evocation of Hell, that Arnall's precepts are aimed directly at him.

Early in the chapter, Stephen is clearly distinguished from his schoolmates. His friends react to the tired pun on Lawless's name with subdued laughter, but Stephen, uneffected by Arnall's efforts at grim levity, finds his emotions shrivelling up and shrinking away. The more superficially cosmopolitan Heron hums his ditties, but Stephen can see only the horror of the approaching religious exercises.

The "retreat", from the world of materialism into a contemplation of the spiritual life, accomplishes the opposite of its purpose: its errors, both doctrinal and emotional, eventually lead Stephen from the Church. In addition, the subject matter of the sermons has little to do with spirituality. The Retreat Sermon resembles the preachment of Father Purdon in "Grace." And Purdon Street was in the center of Dublin's brothel district.

ST. FRANCIS XAVIER. The retreat is held in honor of St. Francis Xavier—historically, because he was a Jesuit, and symbolically, because in many ways Xavier's career parallels Stephen's own. St. Francis Xavier was a brilliant student, not a "farcical pedagogue," who left the Parisian world of letters for the more spiritually efficacious life of the priesthood. Stephen probably noticed Arnall's implication that writing and teaching in a secular setting are definitely inferior to a career as God's minister, and even "suspect." Stephen, of course, goes to Paris (among other places) after the close of *A Portrait*.

Essentially, Stephen models one large aspect of his plans for the future upon Xavier's career: St. Francis Xavier brought the gospel of formal religion to heathens; Stephen will preach the gospel of art to the unbelieving Philistines. Xavier's arm became paralyzed baptizing so many pagans; Stephen, too, will suffer for his aesthetic beliefs, using his hand to pen his gospel.

Implied in references to St. Francis Xavier is the controversy concerning who should write the Sacred Book for Ireland. During the Irish Renaissance, Celtic authors often used the Biblical analogy of the Jews' enslavement to the Egyptians to delineate their own situation with regard to the British. Many Irish writers felt that their country's Messianic role should be etched in print, and George Moore, in his trilogy, *Ave, Salve, Vale*, believed that he had created Ireland's great prophetic work. *A Portrait* fits unobtrusively into this blending of religion, literature, and politics during the Irish Revival.

STEPHEN IN HELL. Because so many of the vices detailed by the lugubrious Arnall apply directly to Stephen's "sins," he feels his tiny artificial world crumbling under the vehemence of the Retreat Sermon. Stephen comes to judge abhorrent many of the very qualities which have sustained him.

Arnall seems to attack directly Stephen's false pride; his scorn for humble but holy believers; his intellectual rebelliousness, which has made him fall, as did Lucifer, from the sight of God; his refusal to obey God's law, a crime that drove Adam from the Garden of Eden; and his inability to control a lower nature, resulting in his nameless revels and (mostly imagined) orgies.

Some of Arnall's barbs are more subtly related to deeds that Stephen can apply specifically to his own crimes. Arnall excoriates the whitened sepulchers, who hide their iniquities under the cover of holiness: Stephen, as sodality prefect, is expected to set an example of piety during the retreat. Stephen's dread of his sins being revealed must have been heightened by Arnall's allusions to the General Judgment, on the last day. Then his soul would be stripped naked before all whom he had deceived: prefects, companions, and parents, alike. The thought that others may have committed equally heinous acts does not occur to him.

With his tender conscience, then, Stephen applies to himself the full force of Arnall's general reproaches and sees in the lecturer's broadly allusive materials specific crimes of his own past. Caught up in worldly ambition, Stephen finds that the retreat teaches him to question all mundane values, whether they be sex, writing, or intellectual superiority. He finds that the pious demeanor and prayerful ways of his family are methods ordained by God for his salvation and that he is triply damned for denigrating them. Hell, according to Arnall, is composed partly of the chaos stemming from violations of family hierarchy. There the eminently selfish demons scream and thrash about, aware only of their pain, not caring for those to whom they may have been related during life. Stephen sees Arnall's description of the parricide's execution as applying to his own treatment of his family and his country. Alienating himself from the Church through serious sin, Stephen feels that he has morally defiled his trusting family.

From the start of *A Portrait*, Stephen has been preoccupied with the horror of death, picturing Little's death at Clongowes, and relating his own possible death in the infirmary to Parnell's demise. During the Retreat Sermon Arnall presses this nerve, and it is not until the end of *A Portrait* that Stephen finds a partial "answer" to mortality in the Eucharistic nature of his writing.

So powerful is Arnall's description of death that Stephen imagines that he has actually died. The ghostly fingers and the tongues of flame that seem to destroy his physical body later become metamorphosed into weapons employed in Stephen's quest for sacramental meaning in his human creativity. During the retreat, however, the ghostly fingers do not suggest the inspiration of an anthropomorphized Holy Spirit, and the tongues of flame are simply objective correlatives for the hell which Arnall is putting Stephen through.

Worse than the fear inculcated by the Retreat Sermon is the sense of boundless shame which smothers Stephen's soul, making him feel responsible for imagined dire crimes. Forgetting his physiological needs, Stephen believes that he has desecrated Emma by thinking lustfully of her. Regressing, he sees himself and Emma as two children wandering blissfully in the happy state of pre-puberty. Stephen must symbolically castrate himself to be accepted by God and the Virgin Mary.

OBSESSIVE FATHER ARNALL. Father Arnall's ponderous rhetoric, especially adapted to young minds by two centuries of Jesuit polemical methods, proceeds from both his own neurosis and the schizophrenic nature of formal Dublin Catholicism. *Arnall is an obsessive man, using the pulpit to exorcise his own demons.* He is assisted, of course, by such traditional descriptions of Hell as Pinamonti's *Hell Opened to Christians, to Caution Them from Entering into It* (Joyce's main source for the Retreat Sermon); yet he manages to out-Herod Herod.

Father Arnall is a jaded but wily figure, who draws upon the best (or worst) of rhetorical devices. With his rheumy voice and shaking, clasped hands, he resembles one of the devils that he describes so fully. He knows how to appeal to the masses with his simplistic, highly pictorial, and florid sentences. And Arnall is not averse to pitting one student against another. Besides the weak joke at Lawless' expense, he insists that the sodality prefects insure the piety of the other schoolboys during the retreat.

Despite his assured air, however, Arnall is unable to hide his ignorance and his inability to examine old strictures and tired platitudes. He is often trite, and speaks of the "name and fame" of St. Francis Xavier, not bothering to excise the silly rhyme.

Arnall shares the anti-feminism of the Church, which sees Eve as the prime cause of man's fall. C.S. Lewis might sympathize with this view, but Lewis has the wit to term Adam's demise the first premeditated murder. Arnall blandly states in a sentence that Eve bit the apple and then gave Adam a piece.

Interestingly enough, Arnall sees Adam's lack of moral courage, his inability to resist the temptress, as the main reason for his spiritual death. Stephen may have retained Arnall's depiction of the siren call of women when he penned his villanelle in Chapter Five. One episode of *Ulysses* compares Dublin bar girls to the Sirens who confounded the Greek prototype.

Given his untested view of the Church's attitude towards women, it is not surprising that Arnall lays the full blame for Christ's Crucifixion on the Jews—though the doctrine is retained by the Catholic Church.

ARNALL'S PROJECTIONS. Arnall's personal obsessions are especially noticeable when he discusses two concepts at the heart of Christianity: physical death and the lesser importance of man's lower nature when compared with his immortal soul. Arnall saves his most vehement sermonizing for his description of the physical facts of death. *His impassioned, masochistic views may impress terrified youngsters*—and they do intimidate Stephen—*but upon reflection his concepts are replete with errors.* Arnall's depiction of death is disgusting; it is also illogical.

It is difficult to reconcile Arnall's picture of the filthy, quivering, protoplasmic blob that the dead body soon becomes with his other stated belief that the body is the tabernacle of the Holy Ghost. Indeed, the Church believes so strongly in the resurrection of the body, in its inviolability even after the soul has left, that it bans cremation. In his sermon Arnall exaggerates Church teaching, which euphemistically explains that man will return to dust, and places himself definitely on the side of decay. It is unfortunate for Stephen that an authority figure with such a pronounced "death wish" can exert so much influence on sensitive young men.

Arnall's views of the lower man are correlatives of his obsession with death. So vividly does he picture the snares of the flesh that his exhortations partake of Manicheanism, which sees man's emotions as stemming from an evil Principle in the universe and which insists that the passions must be ruthlessly suppressed. Arnall's view of the instincts are partly Jansenistic as well, stressing as they do a complete reliance on the ascetic.

In all of this *it is clear that Arnall is projecting his own attempts at sexual repression onto a body of Church doctrine* which at least tries to balance conflicting aspects of human nature. Arnall is an unbalanced grotesque, but his words do convince the ingenuous (for a time). *Much of what he says can be found in Jesuit retreat manuals dating back to the Sixteenth Century.*

ARNALL'S SCRIPTURAL ERRORS. In order to substantiate his pessimistic views, Arnall wrenches passages of Scripture from context, completely distorting their meaning. Often the contexts of the quotations counsel mercy or argue to a regenerative view of human nature. Arnall sees little of God's compassion in his Biblical sources.

On a few occasions, *Joyce permits Arnall to make factual errors* in his Scriptural citations. The most famous of these is his allusion to *Ecclesiastes 7:40* in the opening lines of his first sermon, in which he exhorts his audience to consider the "last things" as a prophylactic against sin: in reality, the quotation comes from *Ecclesiasticus 7:40*. Joyce, a careful writer, certainly includes the errors consciously (after all, Bloom, in *Ulysses*, lives on Eccles St.) in order to heighten *the irony of the intelligent Stephen's victimizing by academic as well as moral incompetents.*

Arnall's designation of the world as "wretched" is appropriate to his own psyche; and his entreaty to those making the retreat to "help" him has more validity than he realizes.

OTHER BLUNDERS. Other errors in Arnall's lectures become evident upon a rereading of the text and, in Stephen's case, upon a rethinking of the issues. Arnall preaches a cash-dime theory of salvation, which amounts to simony: good deeds earn the best interest in God's bank. He glibly assumes that the soul is judged the instant that death occurs and apparently has given little thought to a valid definition of the moment of death. He repeats the tired Catholic maxim that Mary is more approachable by sinners than the "offended" Godhead without wondering about the reverse priority that makes a Mother more amenable to favors than her Son. He recites the trite parable of the Garden of Eden, specifying its location and landscaping. Arnall states that water as well as blood came from Christ's pierced side, ignorant as he is of the possible scientific validation of the Crucifixion: the water may have been lymph.

Arnall's huckstering is often counter-productive. The hackneyed test of placing a finger in flames to conceive of the pains of Hell has not led many children to God. And Arnall's variation of Blaise Pascal's famous "bet" (itself stemming from St. Augustine) succeeds only if unexamined. Augustine rhetorically asked what a man gained if he possessed the world but lost his soul, and Pascal counseled his Jansenistic followers to make a holy wager: Give up, he advised, the mixed blessings and curses of life for a chance at an immortal existence. In Chapter Five Stephen reverses Pascal's bet and rejects Augustine's implication. He places his "bet" firmly on this life, believing in the possibilities of man and taking a chance on losing eternity.

In short, things are not always most intense at their centers, as Arnall maintains—witness a hurricane; a venial sin is not as evil as Arnall pretends—Aquinas maintains that one need not be explicitly confessed; and Christ is not wounded daily by our sins.

One can forgive Arnall for his inability to reconcile God's perfect justice with his perfect mercy, to see as one the blood of Jesus, the Innocent Lamb, and the blood demanded by the Jesus who exacts retribution. Joyce was willing, though reluctantly, to see the insolubility of such mysteries and to respect the fine mind of Aquinas, who came as close as anyone to elucidating them. What cannot be forgiven are Arnall's refusal to admit the possible contradictions and the form which he uses to explain them: a cheapening anthropomorphism.

Arnall's description of God's motives is a base slander. He spends little time on the beauty and wonder of God's justice; instead, he portrays him as a miffed patron exacting vengeance upon ungrateful underlings. The constantly repeated adjective "offended" does little to explain God's attitudes. In Arnall's hands, God becomes the ruffled marquis devising a "variety" of tortures for the unrepentant.

ARNALL ON HELL. Father Arnall's picture of Hell is derived from three main sources: arguments from "authorities," such as St. Catherine of Siena, who have supposedly been granted a vision of Hell; a terrifying logic which extends infinitely all the evils encountered in this life; and "composition of place," a method of conjuring up the physical details of a spiritual mystery, its location, etc. The last was used extensively by St. Ignatius Loyola in his meditations. Ignatius found that the mystery of the Annunciation, for example, became more meaningful to him when he tried to picture such concrete objects as Mary's dress and the furnishings in her room when the angel appeared to her. The theory is presented in his *Book of the Spiritual Exercises,* finished in the mid-Sixteenth Century.

Joyce often uses his authorities ironically. Though not quite a father of the Church, Addison is cited as an expert in the art of dying peacefully. Arnall, of course, ignores the fact that Addison, the Tory, was no friend to the Irish and served as secretary to the man who became the Lord Lieutenant of Ireland. The fact that the nasty young Warwick was Addison's stepson, though, may have some relevance to Joyce's father-son theme in *A Portrait.*

Arnall's most interesting authorities include St. Catherine of Siena, who found a devil so ugly that she averred her willingness to walk on hot coals for the rest of her life rather than see one again; St. Anselm, who relates that Hell is so crowded that the condemned will be unable even to pluck a hungry worm from his eye; the unnamed saint who defines an eternity of damnation through the continuous sound of the words "ever" and "never"; and St. Bonaventure, who maintains that the putrid odor of one corpse released from Hell could spread pestilence over the entire world.

The logic of Arnall's Hell is based on two premises: first, since Hell is the absence of all good, i.e., complete evil, all pains in life will be magnified in the Inferno, developed to their utmost limits; secondly, God's omnipotence permits Him to suspend laws which govern temporal suffering. Thus the fire in Hell is dark; and, though it burns with infinite fierceness, it does not consume.

Stephen apparently has no difficulty applying Arnall's tenets of Hell to his own unhappy present existence. The dirt and squalor of his family's home and of the brothel area which he frequented are translated into infernal stench as Stephen visualizes his probable future. Stephen has always had trouble adjusting to his acquaintances; now he is told to imagine sharing all eternity with the most distasteful companions. Again, he has been forever impatient with time, restlessly desiring to meet his ideal image in the real world; now he is faced with the tedium and unhappiness of a never ending world of torment.

The worst suffering in Hell is the pain of loss. Citing Aquinas, Arnall asks his listeners to recall their sadness at the loss of a loved one, then to imagine how they will feel when they have lost infinite goodness forever—God. And added to this torment is the pain of fruitless remorse, heightened by the jeers of the fallen souls who have led the condemned to sin. The prostitutes, who appear to Stephen as harlots bedecked with jewels, scurrying like frightened mice, will mock him for all eternity. Stephen is far from his innocent dreams of Mercedes.

Taken as a whole, the Retreat Sermon is a brilliant example of dramatic irony, a naturalistic, microscopic inspection of a cancerous growth in Roman Catholicism and a revelation of two discrete minds, Father Arnall's and Stephen's, which come together like the indistinguishable flanges of a tongue of flame, only to separate. Stephen will outgrow the exorcism of his spirit by the rheumy Arnall; for the Irish clergy there is only stagnation. Stephen is

soon to see Ireland itself as the cramped Hell described so
vividly by the retreat master.

AFTER HELL. Following Arnall's preaching, Stephen's
trip to Hell, the protagonist reascends to a parody Heaven
of Communion and communication with his fellows. In the
meantime, he travels through a mock Purgatory of evil
visions and a humiliating but temporarily satisfying Confession. Stephen must die to an old way of life; and, after
the Retreat Sermon, he experiences a literal sense of extinc-
tion. His specious resurrection into a period of religious
formalism is contrasted in *A Portrait* with his later rebirth
into a beginning life as an artist. Stephen's fear of immediate death after Arnall's strictures stems in part from
his literal interpretation of the retreat master's assurance
that God is calling to him.

CLONGOWES AND CORK AGAIN. Before confessing,
Stephen unsuccessfully employs the defense mechanisms
that have assisted him in the past. He crawls into bed for
security just as he did when physically sick at Clongowes
and as he will do when meditating upon his villanelle in
Chapter Five. He places his hands over his ears to prohibit
entrance to the dunnings of sexual passion, even as he had
closed his ears at Clongowes to drown out the sounds of
the refectory, another occasion of eating and communicat-
ing. As in Cork, Stephen feels that his room is unreal. At
that time, too, a massive (though transitory) change was
taking place within him.

VISION OF GOATS. *So much has been written about
Stephen's vision of the goatish creatures that it becomes
extremely important to pluck what is worthy from the
dross.* First, Stephen undergoes a vision more than a dream,
and the distinction is significant: Before his death and
ascent into Heaven, St. Stephen, the protomartyr, also
experienced a vision—the skies opened, and he saw his
blissful future. Through Stephen's vision of Hell, Joyce is
both excoriating the morbidity of Arnall and Roman Catholicism and implying that the concept of Hell promulgated
by the Church is no more real than its idea of Heaven.
Both are products of Stephen's overwrought and solipsistic

imagination, feeding upon subject matter provided by false fathers.

Secondly, since Stephen's Hell is the inferno of lust, it appropriately houses goat creatures. As any crusader could testify, who returned from war and found hoof prints under the window of his wife's chamber, the goat for good reasons is considered the symbol of lust, the demon lover. In his trance, Stephen's goats are explicitly compared to the prostitutes that he has been frequenting. Augmenting Stephen's sense of sinning with women is the Church's malignant attitude towards the enticing female.

Other aspects of the vision are more conjectural: Did Joyce consciously use the fact that the thistle is the national emblem of Scotland? Does Joyce employ the color green here, as he does elsewhere in his work, to point up Ireland's decay? Are the canisters knocked about by the demons receptacles for Communion? Do the goat creatures' bony faces suggest the harrowed past of Ireland, with its ravaged historians such as Johnny Cashman? And does the monotonous, whispered language of the creatures foreshadow Stephen's confession to the old Capuchin?

CATAPULTED TOWARDS HEAVEN. Joyce undercuts Stephen's respite following the nightmare vision with subtle irony. Upon awakening, Stephen sees Dublin through a yellowish haze. He appeals to Mary as the morning star, an appellation which, like the expression "Tower of Ivory," is always used sardonically by Joyce. Also, in Stephen's repeated self-admonition to Confess, which contrasts so forcefully with his previous refusals to Admit, Joyce signals the state of moral glibness into which his hero has fallen.

The ironic tone of the last few pages of Chapter Three is most clearly seen in Joyce's contrast between Stephen's spiritual bewilderment and his recurring thoughts of the family's supper. In a sense, Communion will satisfy only a temporary appetite. In these closing pages the snake of Eden becomes explicitly the phallic serpent of lust.

STILL SUPERCILIOUS. Stephen again fails to become one of the "people," even though his external posture suggests a deep sense of humility. He assumes his superiority to the unkempt girls whom he sees on his way to the chapel, even as he reasons that their souls might indeed be more acceptable to God than his. His reactions to the old woman of whom he asks directions are stilted. And his preparation for confession parodies the Publican in the Parable, as he secretly beats his breast, praying for humility. Stephen wants to be like the simple followers of Christ, who mended their nets, and the image suggests Stephen's false capitulation: Later he will fly past society's nets.

STEPHEN'S CONFESSION. Joyce uses fine control in describing Stephen's confession to the old Capuchin as he suggests the worthlessness of the formal rite of Penance. The priest does not scold Stephen or drive him from the confessional with exclamations of disgust. Instead, in his tired and platitudinous way, he tries to help the bedeviled child. So superficial is his counsel, however, that his false piety leads to Stephen's conviction in Chapter Four that the life of a priest is one of rigid order and little inspiration.

Joyce condemns the Irish clergy by having the old Capuchin ask one question of Stephen's dealings with the prostitutes: Were they married? The theological point is that breaking the Ninth Commandment, "Thou shall not covet thy neighbor's wife," is more evil than offending against the Sixth, "Thou shall not commit adultery." The more important point is that Stephen will soon see how completely irrelevant the priesthood is to his own aspirations.

Joyce's *economic use of details* sets the scene for the ritual. The candles have been extinguished, and one is reminded of the bleak ending of "Araby," in which the silence of the darkened bazaar is said to resemble that of a church after the lights have gone out. Again, as he waits his turn, Stephen imagines the burning cities destroyed by God because of their inhabitants' sexual transgressions; the implied reference to sodomy helps define his own sense of shame and horror. Finally, the meaningless formality of the Sacrament is objectified in the opening and shutting of the confessional's panels.

Joyce captures well the emotions of a young Catholic about to relate to another person's crimes which he considers heinous. Stephen knows that the other penitents will become aware of his lengthy confession. He begins his recital by minor sins, perhaps experiencing the shame felt by the apocryphal Catholic lad who reserved the worse part of his confession for the period when the passing street car would drown out his words. Stephen exhausts his store of venial offenses, even the nebulous vice of sloth; then there is no hope: he must admit his violations against purity.

A skillful confessor might have reassured Stephen that his faults were not unique, but such understanding clerics were not and are not to be found in large numbers. Instead, the well-meaning Capuchin uses the same fear tactics as did Father Arnall. Though he expunges Stephen's immediate sins, he gives him little to go on in the future— after the fear (and exhilaration) have worn off. The Capuchin's words are a brief shower falling upon the desert of Stephen's spirit, but the water soon evaporates.

Through the use of the color white, Joyce implies that Stephen's spiritual state after Confession is not so much pure as pallid. The white rose, the white pudding, the white flowers at the altar, and the pale flames of the candles all indicate that true life and fulfillment have been flushed out of Stephen's personality. The eggs which he looks forward to after Mass betoken no permanent Resurrection.

The chapter ends on a note of "inflation," as Stephen identifies himself comfortably with a group for the first time in the novel. Unfortunately, his new world is as full of bravado as Miranda's.

CHAPTER FOUR

MECHANICS OF RELIGION. Joyce describes Stephen's new state of grace in terms of mathematics. The image of Stephen's ringing up indulgences on a great Heavenly cash register has been widely noted by critics, but Stephen's brittle and transitory sanctification is defined as well by several other references to the sterile ethic which he has imposed upon his unwilling soul. In the opening pages of the chapter, Stephen is deeply involved in the paraphernalia of penances and indulgences and in a watered down version of medieval allegory which consigns the logic of the Schoolmen to the narrow confines of the catechism. At one point, Stephen's relationship with God is described as a theorem.

The opening paragraph of Chapter Four sets the tone for Stephen's surface conversion; each holy item is formally assigned a separate day for discussion and meditation. Stephen tries to align his soul with the choplogic of the Church and spends hours brooding over distinctions among the Seven Gifts of the Holy Ghost; and, although he cannot tell apart Wisdom, Understanding, and Knowledge, he is convinced that the Seven Gifts will cleanse him of the Seven Deadly Sins in his past. Equally fruitless are Stephen's bewilderment over the religious significance of the number three and his inane thumbing of the rosary beads.

In *Finnegans Wake,* Joyce was to use such numbers to pen his eminently humane document and was to compare the book's structure to a rosary; but such pious externals have little permanent influence on Stephen's spiritual state. The symmetry which Stephen perceives in the relationship of God to his creation is simply unfulfilling: The universe becomes a vast requiem for the hero, and he muses that his death will make little difference to God.

CONFUSED THEOLOGY. Stephen's anxieties at the start of Chapter Four stem in part from his overreaction to the confusing precepts of his masters. Stephen is unable to see that one may *feel* nothing towards God or things religious and yet *be* in the state of grace. Seen doctrinally, spiritual dryness is often God's test of the soul; but Stephen, whether through artistic sensibility or through a touch of neurosis, refuses to accept this incomplete state. Perhaps he has been told by the clerics that illumination will come in this life, after he has exercised the proper religious muscles.

Stephen's continuing imperfections and his inability to experience joy in prayer lead him into endless worries about the state of his soul. As do many Catholic boys, he wonders whether his sins have truly been forgiven, then, in a dreadful distortion of reason, concludes that God must have been obliged to provide the grace needed to resist temptation. Again, he pitifully relies upon the tired Church maxim that temptation is proof of the soul's remaining pure.

SATIRE. Joyce gains aesthetic distance, ie., puts space between himself and Stephen, by his slight parody of the protagonist. The satiric treatment here of a youth who once shared traits of Joyce himself is somewhat cruel, but the comic description of Stephen's foibles does permit a measure of objectivity. Thus we are told that Stephen finds mortification of the sense of smell the most difficult task of all, probably because he is used to bodily odors—Joyce hated to wash—and we discover that Stephen persistently musters all of his inventiveness to devise intricate ways of mortifying his sense of touch. This sense, of course, he has offended by consorting with prostitutes.

STEPHEN'S SENSITIVITY AGAIN. Many of Stephen's problems in these pages stem from the artistic sensibility which he has retained through the execrable retreat. His imaginative view of reality consistently struggles with the theological formalism that he is urged to adopt. As he attends a gloomy early Mass, he sees himself as a catechumen, and the light of his imagination glimmers through the dark of the catacomb as he listens to the mutter of the priest. The prayers which he mechanically tries to recite on his beads fade into disembodied essences. He is more enamoured of the mysterious Procession of the Holy Ghost from the Father and the Son than by the doctrinal absolute that God has loved his soul for all eternity. He wonders what the Sin against the Holy Ghost, the one unforgivable sin, might be; and it is appropriate that during his illumination at the chapter's end the wading girl is described as a dove.

Stephen's imaginings about religion are epitomized in the word "swoon"; and his ecstasy partakes of that mingling of adoration and repressed passion experienced by the narrator of "Araby." Stephen also shares this lad's attachment to dog-eared tomes of theological arcana. His readings in St. Alphonsus Liguori are exhilarating, both sexually and spiritually, though he would never admit the presence of the former passion.

MORE SKULLS AND CROSSBLINDS. *Stephen's meeting with the Director is extremely rich in symbolic meaning* and has been explicated at length by several Joyceans. In a position of mock Crucifixion, the priest leans on the cross-blind, the term implying both that the Director is blind to the true meaning of the Cross and that he may use the Cross to blind Stephen to his real vocation. The noose which he ties represents the seductive nature of the priesthood, which exalts by providing the powers to consecrate bread and to forgive sin, but which debases the individual by imposing a rigid order upon his spirit. The waning light, then, objectifies Stephen's fading belief in formal religion.

CLONGOWES, AGAIN. The scene looks back to the young Stephen's meeting with Conmee: Joyce refers to the Director's skull, to Stephen's desultory examination of more portraits, and to the omnipresent swish of a soutane. With the deliberately stilted phrase, the "message of summons," Joyce foreshadows Stephen's real summons by the bird-girl at the end of the chapter.

LES JUPES. The discussion of the Capuchins' billowing skirts, *les jupes,* serves several purposes. It lightly hints at clerical transvestitism; it reveals the Director's attempt to denigrate a rival religious order—witness Simon Dedalus' early advocacy of the Jesuits over the Christian Brothers—; and it provides the material for the Director's sly testing of Stephen.

Stephen refuses to be drawn into revealing his true attitude towards the insinuating Director's patronizing comments about the Dominican's habits. Owing to his adopted mask of humble obedience, he ruminates to himself about the sexual connotation of skirts. Sitting in the dark, the Director resembles an interrogator loosed upon a shackled prisoner. Already, however, Stephen is learning to use the weapons of silence, exile, and cunning. His cause for emotion is profound, since his cleansing confession of the previous chapter was heard by a Capuchin; yet he is able to hold his tongue.

CESSATION OF HOSTILITY. Stephen's attitude towards the clergy here is one of pity, not open scorn. Both his maturity and his independence are seen in his tired thoughts of wearying clerics who teach that Macaulay never committed a deliberate mortal sin—obviously, all mortal sins are deliberate, requiring consent of the will—and who prefer the pale writing of Louis Veuillot to the vibrant products of Victor Hugo. For the time being, at least, Stephen has lost the militancy that inspired him to fight for the cause of Byron over Tennyson.

THE TEMPTATION. Arnall had appealed to Stephen's sense of shame during the Retreat Sermon; the Director appeals to his pride. The Director offers power of all types, and one is reminded of the catechetical question asked of Irish children during Joyce's time: "If you saw an angel and a priest walking towards a church door, for which one would you open it first?"; and the answer: "For the priest, for only he can consecrate the bread and wine into the body and blood of Christ."

Joyce delineates several reasons that priesthood might entice Stephen, and Stephen's musings are remarkably self-revelatory. He reasons that ordination would provide him with the ritual needed to escape from the life of humble worshippers. On the altar, somewhat below the celebrant (who must assume responsibility), Stephen can lose himself in a vague world of Latin rubrics, divorced from the real world of pious believers. Decked out in strange garments, Stephen will have his aloofness condoned sacramentally. In addition, ordination will separate Stephen from sins, and he will even return, with God's grace, uncontaminated from the confessional.

Stephen's other motives are less profound: the priesthood will provide a ritualistic antedote to his sloth, grant him the key to secret knowledge, and permit him access to the whispered blemishes of women in the confessional.

LEAVING THE CHURCH. *Because the entire novel is a statement of why Stephen leaves behind formal Catholicism, Joyce spends little time explaining his motivation at this time. Significantly, though, for Stephen, deciding not to be a priest is tantamount to resolving not to be a practicing Catholic.*

Although Stephen himself does not know exactly why he rejected the Director's offer of Holy Orders, he does have some beginning insight into his motives. First, Stephen superimposes upon his imagined future as a priest his execrable past at Clongowes. Unlike other students, Stephen was able to see through the comfortable facades of his bleary masters, and he does not want such a life for himself. Also, he is repelled by the quasi-military order— a pun which appears throughout the pages—of priestly organizations; and, though he knows that ordination offers security, he would rather take his chances in the real world of pitfalls and labyrinths.

More subtle is Stephen's perception of himself as a fallen being; he feels that he is not physically constituted to withstand temptation, and he does not wish to waste his life's energy upon a losing war with the devil.

HOME AGAIN. Stephen's perception of his family's poverty and his sense of guilt over being the member of the family who has been given all the advantages reinforce his conviction that the world of the clergy is unreal. Momentarily, his universe becomes furnished with the twisted statue of Mary amidst poor cottages, the odor of rotted farm produce, a stranger who plunges a spade into the earth, and a dishevelled but loving family, with its weak tea, perpetual relocations, and sentimental lyrics from Thomas Moore.

As he listens to the singing of his siblings, Stephen experiences a true epiphany, perceiving in the melody of cold and hungry children the weariness of all children from all time. He becomes one with Matthew Arnold in "Dover Beach," with Faulkner's Dilsey and Benjy, and with Cardinal Newman, who finds hope of rebirth in suffering. Blatty was to use Newman in a similar way in *The Exorcist,* whose central theme is that, though the demons want us to see only the dirt of human nature, there is much beauty behind the appearances.

LETTING GO. Stephen, appropriately, paces between Byron's publichouse and Clontarf Chapel before beginning his excursion. Byron has been a consistent symbol of liberation from the start of *A Portrait,* and Clontarf Chapel suggests the dual call of religion and nationalism. The Battle of Clontarf, in which the Irish defeated the Danes, began on Good Friday in 1014. The fact that Clontarf means the "field of the bull" blends with Stephen's appelation, "Bous Stephanoumenos," "ox-wreathed."

The start of Stephen's imaginative voyage shows him breaking away: he perceives in his mother's skepticism about his decision to enter college the divergence of views which will be expanded in Chapter Five; and he looks upon his prospective entrance into the university as an adventure. The triple flame which he imagines will not grace a Christian altar; rather, Stephen envisions a humanistic, even pagan future at the Catholic college. His contemplation of elves and lively, hidden woodland creatures suggests Pan more than Christ. Buoyant in his sense of an open future, Stephen can feel only pity and shame for the "squad" of Christian Brothers who march across the symbolic bridge, in the opposite direction. They apparently hear a different drummer.

INTOXICATION OF WORDS. Stephen knows what he does *not* want, a life of religion, but he has yet to learn specifically what he *does* want from life. As he walks towards his illumination, he experiences the ecstasy which comes from shuffling off the coils of a past life. He has had his spiritual bad tooth extracted and is still intoxicated by the ether: naturally, he is drunk on words.

Stephen's movement is not towards the outside world; he has forgotten for a time the call to duty heard in his family's singing of Moore's *Melodies;* and, though he loves words for their rhythm and color, he sees them primarily as means to express his own inner turmoils, methods to impose order upon his individual chaos. Floating upon the waves of self-induced exhilaration, Stephen feels both hope and despair. He sees Dublin as a bonded slave to many conquerors, including the Danes, and looks for solace to the clouds drifting to the west of Ireland: they have beheld the liberated expanses of Europe.

He rejects, too, the world of nude, swimming youngsters, whose boisterousness, he feels, cloaks their terror at their own bodies. Stephen is not yet ready to plunge into life; and one is reminded of the first chapter of *Ulysses*, in which Buck Mulligan dives into Dublin Bay while Stephen, associating water with drowning, watches the sea from the beach.

STEPHEN'S ANALOGUES. *Many critics have been bothered by the possible overwriting* in the last few pages of Chapter Four, calling the description of Stephen's enlightenment Paterian and Shelleyan and arguing that there is no basis for Joyce's comparison of Stephen to the Resurrected Christ. These same critics also sight the sometimes confused Daedalian imagery in the novel, culminating in Stephen's vision of the winged form ascending the air.

From a negative viewpoint, Joyce seems to have projected upon Stephen's flight from the Church his own paranoia; positively, however, he seems to have expanded a small romantic part of himself, which remained unmitigated by the cares of the real world, into the supple and deeply poetic delineation of Stephen's change. The pages may be Paterian, but they certainly rival the best of Pater. Again, though, the corrective of irony is not apparent upon a first reading of the novel; and the pages, which at least border on sentimentality, have been most popular with beginning students of Joyce.

DEDALUS. Stephen's perception of Daedalus as the "fabulous artificer" suggests his wish to pattern his artistic life upon his Greek namesake's ability to impose order on vague myths. The fable of Daedalus will replace the *mythos* of Catholicism in Stephen's future creative plans. Joyce himself structured his work with stringent architectonics (or "artifices"), and, of course, in *Ulysses* he used mythic materials. Once again, however, it is important to distinguish between Joyce's artistic processes and Stephen's unformed enthusiasm.

Stephen's vision of Daedalus implies, too, his initiation into a priestly rite that goes far beyond the Irish and their legends of victory over Danish (or English) invaders. Stephen will seek access not to priestly secrets but to the clandestine underpinnings of classical times. No longer will he look to Rome, but, instead, will seek truths, albeit half-truths, from the oracles of Delphi and the whispering reeds of Pan.

Merging with the Daedalian image, Stephen no longer fears the once threatening eagles. Like Shelley's skylark, he wishes to burst forth in song but to do so from a height, soaring alone with one cry, above mere mortals. Much of this romanticism, however, will be undercut by the prosaic, "deflated" beginning of the next chapter.

STEPHEN'S RESURRECTION. The Christocentric symbolism in the pages is harder to accept, especially since Joyce confuses his allusions, having Stephen undergo his Transfiguration and Resurrection on one page—and in reverse order. The latter is denoted by allusions to "cerements," Christ's burial clothing, which was folded neatly by the empty tomb on Easter Sunday. At this point, Stephen's "mission" differs from that of the risen Christ: Stephen seeks solitude; Christ worked through his disciples. For a while Stephen is enjoying the splendid isolation of his pagan ordination; in the next chapter, he will gather together a band of mock apostles.

A LADY IN WADING. Several critics have pointed out that Stephen's vision of the bird-girl represents his Baptism into a life of creativity. The Biblical parallel is with the Baptism of Christ in the Jordan by John the Baptist. Then, the Holy Ghost in the form of a dove appeared in the sky to signal God the Father's approval of his Son's mission. Here, Joyce indicates the reference by allusions to the dove; to ivory, which has been associated throughout the novel with the Blessed Mother; and, of course, to the blue of the girl's skirts—Mary's color. Also, the expression, "a sign upon the flesh," lends a general Biblical tone to the passage.

It seems, though, that *other levels of symbolism in the section are just as important as the somewhat confused Biblical analogies*. Looking out to sea, the girl is gazing towards the liberated territory of Europe, to which Stephen will soon venture. But she is also a Siren, complete with a green trail of seaweed, and Stephen must be wary of this mermaid, who may well bind him to the little green place called Ireland—or perhaps upset his curragh should he look back at her while he is journeying abroad. Stephen, then, is Telemachus at the start of his trip, even as he is in the first chapter of *Ulysses*. In *A Portrait* Stephen never does immerse himself in water, and the novel ends with his preparation to cross over into Europe.

The girl represents, too, the appeal of sensuality, which Stephen later realizes that he must avoid if he is to devote himself fully to art. Unlike the other females in the novel, *for the most part mere symbolic figments that hurry across Stephen's mind,* this girl is fully fleshed. Stephen's profane joy stems from his vision of her as both a living, "girlish" creature and as a person who has the added allure of being beyond shame or wantonness. In a sense, however, Stephen is projecting his newly found freedom onto a common girl who is simply kicking the water about.

As in his vision of Emma after the cathartic of Confession, Stephen feels that with such a girl he could walk blamelessly through life. Joyce, though, has added the element of sex to Stephen's adolescent craving for a guiltless emotional attachment. The bird-girl is Emma, with sex appeal.

TURNING ASIDE. It is significant that Stephen does not communicate with the girl, except through his eyes (as Bloom will do with Gerty MacDowell in the Nausicaa Episode of *Ulysses*); the girl simply acts as catalyst for his dormant emotions. She has, however, provided him with a small insight into what can be experienced through a Heavenly being, who combines religion and the underlying sexual passions of Ireland's peasants.

Running off, Stephen sleeps deeply, enthralled by a sense of personal harmony with the universe—not the mechanical order of a theistic plan which once made him feel that his death would go unnoticed. Stephen has experienced a sense of things being "freely given"—to quote the Existentialists. In "The Dead" Gabriel Conroy underwent a massive epiphany just before falling asleep in the Gresham Hotel. The insight of the older Gabriel, though, was profoundly pessimistic. Stephen, Joyce wishes us to believe, will go on to create life, to consecrate the daily bread of experience into an imperishable essence.

No matter that his emotions will not last or that there is really little substance in his vision, *Stephen's perception of the bird-girl is nevertheless his high point in the novel.*

Joyce delineates Stephen's temporary mastery of his destiny by his description of the new moon as an almost buried silver hoop. Stephen, for the moment, has risen above this celestial body, whose presence up to now has symbolized his earth-bound insecurity; and he has all but "buried" his priestly chalice. Chapter Five will describe his attempts to complete the process.

CHAPTER FIVE

DEFLATION. The opening of Chapter Five shows the young Icarus brought down to earth, the description suggesting decay and dislocation: inadequate food; an inaccurate clock; louse marks; the dark pool of the jar, which resembles the pool that Stephen waded through in Chapter Four to secure illumination; and Stephen's whistling and cursing father.

HOLY WEEK SERVICES. C. G. Anderson has traced the Holy Thursday Mass in Chapter Five. Stephen, Anderson maintains, is now a priest of art and performs the appropriate rite. In Anderson's analysis, the tea and crusts become the matter for Communion, with the pawntickets the actual wafers; Stephen is "purified" by his mother, and the triple invocation of Jesus by the mad nun ends the Mass.

Joyce was attracted by the Holy Week services, which exemplified to his mind the drama of a Man about to be betrayed by his friends but who persists in his designs. In Stephen's case, though, the parallel does smack of sentimentality—or of an irony which is too heavy.

DAVIN. In contrast to the shadowy literary figures which Stephen has chosen to lose himself in, Davin is a flesh and blood creature, dull but real. Then, too, he has an infectious warmth missing in Stephen, who spends his time meditating upon summaries of St. Thomas and Aristotle and seeking to nurture the delicate grace of the Elizabethan lyric. Davin's guilelessness is a welcome contrast to Stephen's priggishness and lassitude, and Joyce may have gone too far with his ironic undercutting of the protagonist.

Though Stephen finds some basic worth in Davin, the young Ibsenite looks condescendingly upon the stalwart peasant who worships Ireland's past. The nationalistic Davin has been schooled in the Gaelic League, and Stephen sees, in his credulous attitude towards the frequently garbled versions of Ireland's folklore and mythology, the posture of an Irish serf who has simply added to the shackles of Roman Catholicism the bondage of an equally fabulous prehistory.

DAVIN'S TALE. The topless peasant woman who asks Davin in for the night represents Ireland herself, who has always invited the invading stranger to her bed, whether he be Dane or English. Joyce associates her with all Irish women, who try to break loose from their sexual repressions and the tyranny of the Church. Her milk, her possible pregnancy, and her straightforwardness suggest her underlying ability to offer emotional fulfillment to a paralyzed country.

THE DEAN OF STUDIES. Joyce's irony is again ~~uble~~-edged, used to satirize Stephen's stilted querulous- ~~and~~ the Dean's inanity. Stephen glibly quotes Aquinas' ~~that~~ the good is that which pleases, while reducing ~~ieval~~ philosopher's thoughts to methods that may prove useful to him at the moment but which he may barter away when they no longer apply to his life. He quickly dismisses Epictetus and later abruptly calls the priest away from his musings on the word, "tundish."

The Dean is a tired follower of Ignatius, crippled like the founder of the Jesuit order, but not possessed of Loyola's fiery zeal: He is cautious not to use too much coal in his own, small fire.

Stephen's victory over the Dean is a linguistic triumph. This English invader calls the famous implement a "funnel," misunderstands Stephen's use of the word, "detain," and speaks in trite figures of speech throughout the episode. Although the Dean calls for a slight draught to assist his flames, his mind is a closed chamber.

Even though the Dean is characterized through Stephen's pontifical viewpoint, he does represent Joyce's attitude towards some of his former religious teachers at University College, Dublin. The Dean constantly advises Stephen not to delve too deeply into literature or philosophy and counsels practicality joined with the accepting spirit of Epictetus. He warns Stephen that his lamp of wisdom may become filled to overflowing.

LESSON IN PHYSICS. During the physics lecture Stephen is exposed to the incarnation of the vision which he beheld in the anatomy theatre in Cork. Here the rude, physical student carving his initials becomes the stage Irishman, Moynihan, whose vulgar remarks are as distasteful to Stephen as the cool, efficient query of MacAlister, who asks which material will be on the test. In the contrast between Moynihan and MacAlister is seen the difference between the two (now formalized) parts of Ireland: the South, with its buffoonery and sentimentality; the North, with its heartless practicality. Joyce acidly heightens the political importance of the scene by the professor's allusion to W.S. Gilbert.

MacCANN. Already living by his artistic code, Stephen refuses to sign MacCann's petition for universal peace: the artist must not be caught by any "net," even one of altruism and fellowship. Stephen's arrogant dismissal of MacCann's plea is balanced by his polite leavetaking, in which he assures the political activist that his signature would have little effect in any case.

Joyce presents dramatically what could have been tedious political debate by shortening the scene, by introducing into it the sycophantic Temple and the strident note of MacAlister, and by having Stephen depart as a mock celebrant of the Mass.

THE NETS. Stephen's declaration to Davin that he will fly past the nets of faith and fatherland and his famous depiction of Ireland as the old sow who devours her litter are placed in dramatic context. The idealistic Stephen is contrasted with the leering Temple, with the forthright but sometimes intemperate Cranly, and with the physical Lynch (named after the mayor of Galway, who hanged his own son), who rubs his hands over his groin and opposes his muscular physique to all of life's problems. Also, Stephen is angered when Davin rejects his confessions of past sins. He seems bothered, in addition, by Davin's puzzled reference to Stephen's family name—one which does not sound Irish—and by Davin's suggesting the real reason for Stephen's dropping out of Gaelic class: jealousy of Father Moran in the matter of Emma Clery.

STEPHEN'S AESTHETICS. Stephen's pomposity in his discussion with Lynch, his slighting references to Aquinas, and his use of a few undeveloped ideas from Aristotle seem less insufferable if the protagonist is viewed as a young man striving to attain the vision of harmony which he has elucidated in his theories of art. As if to point the difference between Stephen's evolving passions and his concept of beauty as stasis, or peace, Joyce presents Stephen at the end of the section examining his befuddled emotions upon seeing Emma.

Not enough attention has been given to Joyce's methods of attaining dramatic tension during the discussion. Certainly, Joyce did well to appoint Lynch interlocutor; for, while he acts frivolously, he is not a complete fool—and he does try to understand Stephen despite his longwinded didactics. Also, the flood of banter from Stephen's less profound schoolmates, the constant interruptions by clanking carts and announcements of exam tallies, manifest Stephen's theme that the search for oneness is often hampered by triviality and multitudinousness.

Essentially, Stephen's aesthetics lead to stasis, a state of apprehending in which the mind is arrested by the quiet contemplation of beauty and the emotions stilled. Thus pity does not achieve this end because the onlooker is moved emotionally by the protagonist's suffering. The essence of classical tragedy, then, is to inculcate a sense of terror, not pity. Put into simple terms, if one weeps at the fate of the hero, he is experiencing kinesis—sentimentality, in its basest form. Thus, at a tragedy, one does not cry.

The trouble, then, is to define what universal elements are found in "beauty," the quality necessary for stasis. With female beauty, for example, each nation has its own standards. Such seeming diversity leads Stephen to cite the three attributes which, Aquinas maintains, constitute beauty: wholeness, harmony, and radiance. The third is the most difficult to define; it springs from an apprehension of the *particular* beauty of a *particular* thing—what Scotus (and later, Hopkins) called a being's "thisness."

Translated into art, beauty is seen in three forms: lyric, epic, and dramatic; and several critics have interpreted Joyce's *Portrait*, a personal cry, albeit a lengthy one, as "lyric"; his *Ulysses*, as "epic"; and his *Finnegans Wake*, as "dramatic." The three forms are based upon increasing aesthetic distance, the lyric being eminently subjective; the dramatic, being totally divorced from the author, who sits behind the stage paring his nails as the self-contained action proceeds without him.

Several critics have pointed out that the aesthetic theories are less profound than they first appear. Stephen's stress upon harmony of parts seems more like Henry James than Aquinas, whose concept of God Stephen conveniently leaves out of the picture. Again, the third or dramatic stage seems too much like a mere play or stage presentation. To some, Stephen appears solidly entrenched in the Art-for-Art's-Sake school, an Oscar Wilde, with

Aristotle added. *Stephen's famous description of the artist refined "out of existence," beholding his handiwork, is taken from a letter written by Flaubert in 1857.*

Joyce's view of Stephen as a mock Christ, suffering from the ignorance of his followers, is reinforced by references to Aquinas' *Pange lingua gloriosi* and to the *Vexilla Regis*. And Joyce relates the entire discussion to Stephen's vision in Chapter Four by referring to Emma as a bird.

THE VILLANELLE. Stephen's writing of the well-explicated villanelle stems in part from his unresolved religious conflicts. He attempts to apply to Emma the same faculty of adoration with which he once worshipped the Blessed Mother. Stephen is angered that Emma places him, a priest of the eternal imagination, below Father Moran in her hierarchy of important persons. The villanelle, then, becomes a vehicle for Stephen's consecration of his emotions, a chalice filled with his conflicting passions—one which will rival Father Moran's. Seen in this light, the inflated religious imagery serves to describe what Stephen thinks of his poem—not what Joyce does.

The composition of the villanelle, then, is still another instance of point-of-view writing in *A Portrait,* meant to locate and isolate Stephen's feelings at this stage of his development. It is Stephen who feels that a simple, flirtatious girl is the lure which led the angels to their downfall, that the earth is swung through space for her, like a swaying censer filled with incense, and that she herself embodies blinded Irish womanhood, slowly awakening to a realization of her own being, but still bound by self-imposed religious restraints.

One must ask, though, what Joyce thinks of the present Stephen and then judge how successfully he carries through his artistic intention. Unfortunately, Joyce seems, once again, to have overworked his irony, for the Stephen of the villanelle is simply not worth the trouble of the over two hundred previous pages which have gone into his formation.

Stephen is almost as divorced from actuality as he was years before, and the villanelle manifests the ill effects of his esoteric aesthetics. Stephen awakens dewy-wet, perhaps dampened by a nocturnal emission; he is overly concerned with the sound of words, as opposed to their meaning; he feels that the red rose of his personality has grown pale; he laments in the manner of Shelley that inspiration soon fades; he appeals to Emma as the love sick courtier of "Araby" might have done; he priggishly refers denigratingly to her family background; and he seems obsessed with menstruation.

Stephen's villanelle is, of course, an intricate poem, representing in the realm of original creativity the complexity of Stephen's previous disentangling of aesthetic theories; and, in both instances, Stephen reveals superior intelligence. And, as several critics have noted, the villanelle does draw together many motifs, both conscious and unconscious, which appear throughout the novel.

Unfortunately, however, intellectual superiority, never ending rage against religion, and a condescending attitude towards the common do not by themselves make a great artist. Stephen could never have written *Ulysses*—or *A Portrait*—, for the great writer must be concerned with "life" as well as with the sounds of words. One of the most striking images that the reader retains from Stephen's Proustian habits of composition is that of the monkish youth lying in bed with the blankets pulled up like a cowl around his face.

MORE BIRDS. Stephen's sight of the hovering and darting birds identifies him as a prophet in the vein of Tiresias, Daedalus, and the Egyptian Mercury, Thoth—a bookish and weary prophet, whose mission begins in the National Library. The birds also confirm his future as a rootless wanderer, part of which role is seen in the chasm separating him from the irate Dubliners who protested at the opening of Yeats' *The Countess Cathleen,* on May 8, 1899.

A DESULTORY CONVERSATION. Although disjointed, the ensuing talk among Cranly, Stephen, and some friends does touch upon a few important themes. The dwarfish creature, possibly the issue of incest, points to two aspects of Ireland: its stunted growth and its insularity. Temple's comments broach the paternity theme, a major one in Joyce. And the blasphemous Goggins introduces the figure who became the much more profane Buck Mulligan of *Ulysses*.

EMMA AGAIN. Stephen's attitude towards Emma here smacks of "sour grapes." He cannot dismiss his emotions for her even though he tries to imagine her not as the fair damsel courted through Elizabethan ditties but as a poxed harlot of the Jacobean Age. He mentally dismisses her, bitterly and silently urging her to love a clean-limbed athlete instead of a would-be poet who loathes washing.

GLYNN. *Still another of Stephen's foils*, Glynn is a false Christ, who, as a tutor, suffers the little children to come unto him, but who is unwilling or unable to offer anything of substance to them. He is a real "farcical pedagogue." Finally, the discussion of limbo and God's Providence is also related to the father theme in *A Portrait*.

CRANLY THE CONFESSOR. Despite a few lapses into meretricious semantics, Stephen does reveal his inmost fears to Cranly, and the exchange between the two is honest and moving. Cranly has been described before as a priest hearing confessions, and now the image proves to be justifiable as he elicits many secret truths from Stephen. Stephen, however, does not heed his sound advice, which he sees as another net, just as he refuses to be drawn into Bloom's lair of hospitality in *Ulysses*. Cranly, though well-meaning, is conventional and mediocre and thus serves as another foil—the most important one—to the rebelling Stephen.

Again, the scene is realized dramatically. Stephen suspects that Emma has been flirting with Cranly; he feels cut off from the joys of the upper middle class and ashamed of his own physical appearance; he becomes angry when Cranly treats his *non serviam* in a cavalier way and then insists that his companion refrain from chewing his perpetual figs during the serious discussion; and, in a poignant moment at the end of the episode, he realizes that Cranly is speaking of himself when he asks if Stephen does not fear to be alone and friendless.

The episode with Cranly permits Stephen to clarify his relationships with his friends and convinces him once and for all that he must work out his destiny by himself, with only his three weapons at his disposal.

Stephen's courage is seen in his decision to leave the Church, to take a chance on damnation, in spite of his lingering, residual apprehension that Catholicism might well be valid. For Stephen neither believes nor disbelieves in the Church; he still respects the possibility of union with the God of his boyhood, still feels that Christ may well be divine; he still contrasts the logic of Catholicism with the implausibility of Protestantism; and he fears to receive the Eucharist without the proper dispositions.

Ironically, it is Cranly who turns out to be the doubter in the discussion, and there is some truth in the view that Joyce himself remained a lapsed Jesuit throughout his life.

STEPHEN'S DIARY. It is appropriate that a young man who will soon begin to translate the materials of his own experiences into fiction should keep a diary—a spring diary, at that, one which looks forward to a new cycle of growth, away from the homeland.

Stephen's jottings afford the reader a last glimpse at his fears and ambitions and recapitulate old themes and motifs: Stephen's alienation from his father and from his mother (who becomes, especially in these last pages, representative of the "motherland" of Ireland); his invocation of his symbolic father, Daedalus, at the end of the book; his defense of the heretic, with Bruno of Nola now taking the place of Byron; his scorn of the political sympathies of the Irish; his confused feelings about Emma, with the suggestion that he might actually "like" her; the appeal to him of foreign shores; and his belief in his own Messianic mission.

Stephen's dreams, archetypal in nature, and probably originating in the Collective Unconscious, objectify the forces that might hamper his flight: he must avoid at all costs going to the west of Ireland to search in the red eyes of superstitious Gaelic peasants for Ireland's folkloric past.

Finally, Joyce makes explicit Stephen's role of redeemer (whether comic or not) by establishing Cranly as the "precursor," John the Baptist, of the "severed head," the product of a miraculous conception by aged loins. But even Cranly must be forsaken as Stephen prepares to cross the water.

CRITICISM OF "A PORTRAIT OF THE ARTIST"

The following analysis examines five areas of discussion among Joyceans concerning *A Portrait:* its essential literary qualities, including early reactions to the book; its structure; irony in *A Portrait;* its epiphanies—or lack of them; and the perplexing villanelle, penned by Stephen in Chapter Five. Fuller documentation of the critical sources cited here appears in the Annotated Bibliography.

THE WORTH OF A PORTRAIT. C.G. Anderson includes several early views of *A Portrait* in his Viking Critical Library edition of the novel. These show that a few major literary figures of the day saw a good deal of value in the strange, new novel which confronted them. Ezra Pound, who felt that *A Portrait* was one of the few novels in English that one could read and reread with pleasure, recognized *A Portrait* at once as a permanent classic and cited Joyce's uncompromising, "hard" view of life. To Pound, Joyce was both a literate author and a man who had not lived in the corrupting " 'lap of luxury.' " Pound finds it tragic that Joyce's clear writing was not attended by the Irish, for, he believes, a country's coherent literature reflects its coherent politics.

H.G. Wells, on the other hand, praises the character of Stephen—"One believes in Stephen Dedalus as one believes in few characters in fiction"—but feels some reservations about the book's structure, a "mosaic of jagged fragments." Wells also makes the well-known charge that Joyce, like Swift, has a "cloacal obsession." To Wells, *A Portrait* is a "book to buy and read and lock up, but it is not a book to miss."

Early literary reviews of *A Portrait* praised the genius of a few scenes in the book and cited Joyce's economy of words. In contrast, some of the negative reaction seems quaint to modern critics. *Everyman* called the book "Garbage" and averred that Joyce "would be at his best in a treatise on drains." The *Irish Book Lover* protested that

83

"No clean-minded person could possibly allow it [*A Portrait*] to remain within reach of his wife, his sons or daughters." The *Lover* also proved somewhat unprophetic in predicting that the novel would attain only a "limited circulation," though this view was shared by Edward Garnett, literary adviser to Duckworth and Company, who rejected the "unconventional" *Portrait*. Others complained that *A Portrait* was an unfair attack on Irish schools and that it might lead to increased emigration—opportunities for useful employment, they felt, were definitely available in Ireland.

Recent critics, of course, have assumed the greatness of *A Portrait* and have tried to define the bases of its worth. Although Anthony Burgess feels that the type of student described in Stephen "disappeared [unfortunately] in 1939," he finds the book itself to be "a lyric meditation which is also highly organized, in which symbolism is cunningly planted and even the most casual record of seemingly pointless speech or action proves . . . to have its place in the intricate scheme—there is no slack, no irrelevance." Part of the novel's high suggestiveness is detected by Hugh Kenner in his description of the opening of *A Portrait:* "Mrs. Dedalus playing the piano for her baby tuckoo to dance is a precise and evocative analogue of the relation between the Muse, *das Ewig-Weibliche*, and the artist in primal innocence." Frank O'Connor, believing that *A Portrait* is a "study in differentiation" based on Aquinas and Aristotle, points out that "In reading Joyce, one is reading Literature—Literature with a capital L." All three critical views differ from those of E.M. Forster in his *Aspects of the Novel:* "Joyce has many qualities akin to prophecy and he has shown (especially in the *Portrait of the Artist)* an imaginative grasp of evil. But he undermines the universe in too workmanlike a manner, looking around for this tool or that . . . " Finally, Marvin Magalaner, writing in 1967, cites the relevance of Stephen Dedalus to the contemporary scene, "To protagonists like Bloom and Stephen is assigned the role of self-liberation, and this is the kind of task that students today understand."

STRUCTURE OF A PORTRAIT. Several critics, citing Joyce's interest in the developing foetus of his son, Giorgio—witness the importance of the term in Chapter Two of *A Portrait*—have found in the gestation of Stephen's soul the principal organizational device in *A Portrait*. Ellmann holds that "The atmosphere of biological struggle is necessarily dark and melancholy until the light of life is glimpsed." Burgess' depiction of Stephen's development correlates with Ellmann's: he sees the fundamental symbol in the novel to be one of "a creature trying to escape from the bondage of the grosser elements, earth and water, and learning painfully how to fly." And Sidney Feshbach tries to determine why "the gestation period should be five chapters. . . . "

Some critics have located a three-part structure in *A Portrait*. Applying Stephen's aesthetic theory to his own developing personality, Frank O'Connor writes of *A Portrait*, "It begins with lyrical forms; when he [Stephen] goes to college, it turns into epic; and, finally, when he makes up his mind to leave home (action), it becomes dramatic—the diary form." Harry Levin feels that the novel is "symmetrically constructed around three undramatic climaxes, intimate crises of Stephen's youth." According to Levin, Stephen's three epiphanic moments, "awakening of the body, literary vocation, farewell to Ireland," leave him progressively lonelier and more isolated. Levin points out that Stephen proposes his three weapons, "exile, silence, and cunning," as substitutes for the nets of "nationality, language, religion."

Other Joyceans have treated *A Portrait* more wholistically. Hugh Kenner maintains that "Ego *vs.* authority is the theme of the three odd-numbered chapters, Dublin *vs.* the dream that of the two even-numbered ones." Father Noon holds that in each of the five chapters "there is a more-or-less dominant image (or symbol), a rather pervasive emotion recollected, and at the end a rather marked pause, a stasis in the action of the story." K.E. Robinson divides *A Portrait* in two: "the first unit of structural interior monologue consists of the whole of the novel up to the important break in Chapter 4, and the second, strictly speaking a unit of narrated interior monologue, of the rest of the book." And William York Tindall, in his brilliant analysis of *A Portrait*, describes its technique of inflation-deflation: "After each of his ecstasies, Stephen comes back

to the kitchen, which serves not only as an ironic device
for deflating him but as an image of the reality to which,
if he is to be an artist, he must return."

IRONY IN A PORTRAIT. John V. Kelleher posits so
clearly the problem of defining the limits of Joyce's ironic
treatment of Stephen Dedalus that his statement is worth
quoting at length:

> I remember that when I first encountered
> Stephen Dedalus I was twenty and I wondered
> how Joyce could have known so much about me.
> That is what I mean by the sort of reading the
> book will continue to get, whatever literary fashion
> may decree. Perhaps about the third reading it
> dawned on me that Stephen was, after all, a bit
> of a prig; and to that extent I no longer identified
> myself with him. (How could I?) Quite a while
> later I perceived that Joyce knew that Stephen
> was a prig; that, indeed, he looked on Stephen with
> quite an ironic eye. So then I understood. At least
> I did until I had to observe that the author's glance
> was not one of unmixed irony. There was compas-
> sion in it too, as well as a sort of tender, humorous
> pride.

Kelleher is on firm ground in his belief that Joyce's
attitude towards Stephen is a mixture of sarcasm and
sympathy, for Joyce once said to his friend, Frank Budgen,
"I have been rather hard on that young man." However,
it was not until the publication of *Stephen Hero,* in 1944,
that Joyceans generally acknowledged the complexity of
Joyce's feelings about Stephen, even though early readers
of *Ulysses* were able to detect, with hindsight, some irony
in *A Portrait.*

Hugh Kenner presents the extreme negative picture of
Stephen: "The 'priest of the eternal imagination' turns out
to be indigestibly Byronic. Nothing is more obvious than
his total lack of humour . . . our impulse on being confronted
with the final edition of Stephen Dedalus is to laugh . . ."
Kenner finds that the religious symbolism in *A Portrait* is
usually used to satirize Stephen's aspirations: "The relation
between Stephen and his sanctified namesake, who was

stoned by the Jews after reporting a vision . . . extends to parody as well as parallel." Mark Schorer, in his crucial essay, "Technique as Discovery" (*Hudson Review*, Spring 1948), largely agrees with Kenner: "when Stephen tells us and himself that he is going forth to forge in the smithy of his soul the uncreated conscience of his race, we are to infer from the very quality of the icy, abstract void he now inhabits, the implausibility of his aim." Even Tindall, who tends to deemphasize Joyce's irony in Stephen's characterization, feels compelled to stress the "compassion" which Joyce feels for his protagonist. And Caroline Gordon, who suggests that *A Portrait* "has been misread by a whole generation," maintains that Stephen's rejection of the priesthood in Chapter Four is "the picture of a soul that is being damned for time and eternity caught in the act of foreseeing and foreknowing its damnation."

Although "nonprofessional" Joyceans such as Burgess balance the negative picture of Stephen—"Stephen's theory of aesthetics is original, logical, and totally uncompromising"—one suspects in depressed moments the accuracy of Wayne Booth's suggestion that the degree of irony in Stephen's characterization may be insoluble: "we must conclude that many of the refinements he [Joyce] intended in his finished *Portrait* are, for most of us, permanently lost. . . . For some of us the air of detachment and objectivity may still be worth the price, but we must never pretend that a price was not paid."

Or perhaps we can throw up our hands and enjoy Tindall's splendid pun (reprinted in Anderson's Critical Library Edition) referring to the title of Joyce's early novel: "the portrait of an autist."

EPIPHANIES? Several critics have taken seriously Joyce's concept of the epiphany, although to others the term remains an ambiguous relic of Joyce's early conception of himself as Christ the Creater or Illuminator. Irene Hendry Chayes, for example, feels that "Joyce's work is a tissue of epiphanies, great and small, from fleeting images to whole books, from the briefest revelation in his lyrics to the epiphany that occupies one gigantic, enduring 'moment' in *Finnegans Wake*, running through 628 pages of text and then returning upon itself." Ms. Chayes does offer, however, a common-sense description of Joyce's term: "What Joyce did was give systematic formulation to a common esthetic experience, so common that few others—writers, if not estheticians—have thought it worth considering for its own sake." Florence Walzl defines the religious implications of Joyce's epiphanies: "so in Joyce's view the writer trans- forms real experience into art, having in the process god- like insights into the nature of things, as a result of which his work of art later offers a like experience to the reader." And Father Noon finds a middle ground between those who trace the rubric of Epiphany through all of Joyce's books and those who would abandon it entirely. Noon maintains that in an Epiphanic moment "The observer, here the reader, is at some point jolted to a pause, or stasis, and wonders at the *being* of some commonplace."

THE VILLANELLE. Kenner's view of the villanelle is part of his portrayal of Stephen as unlikable throughout Chapter Five. Kenner points out that Stephen "writes Frenchified verses in bed in an erotic swoon, and is epi- phanized at full length, like Shem beneath the bed clothes, shrinking from the 'common noises' of daylight..." Wayne Booth speaks sardonically of Stephen's "precious villanelle" and asks, "Are we to smile at Stephen or pity him in his tortured longing? Are we to marvel at his artistry, or scoff at his conceit?"

On the other hand, Robert Scholes has advanced the most positive view of the villanelle. Citing Joyce's "reverent attitude toward the creative process," Scholes finds that "The episode of the villanelle provides him [Stephen] with both experience and terminology, locked in such a tight embrace that they produce not a theory but a poem. It is at this point that Stephen ceases to be an esthete and be- comes a poet." According to Scholes, "Mary is the 'Lure of the fallen seraphim.' The poem is addressed, initially at any rate, to her." The villanelle, Scholes believes, ex- presses the "paradox of the Virgin as Temptress..."

Finally, Bernard Benstock explains how Stephen could plausibly write a romantic poem to the somewhat superfi- cial Emma Clery, its ostensible subject. Benstock sees the villanelle as a subjective but valid beginning of Stephen's cultural synthesis.

QUESTIONS AND TOPICS FOR REVIEW AND
FURTHER STUDY

One Hundred Specific Questions on "A Portrait"

Chapter One.

1. Why does Joyce call attention to Stephen's wetting the bed?
2. How do Stephen's problems with Eileen Vance foreshadow his later difficulties with religion and sex?
3. What is the importance of Nasty Roche's question regarding Stephen's father?
4. Why does Joyce use the War of the Roses to define Stephen's participation in Arnall's mathematics class?
5. What indications of Stephen's sensitivity, during his early days at Clongowes, does Joyce provide?
6. How does Stephen try to cope with his bewilderment at Clongowes?
7. How is the Christmas Dinner Scene the beginning of Stephen's "apostasy"?
8. What is the symbolic importance of the Christmas season during the scene?
9. What means does Joyce use to make the Christmas Dinner Scene dramatically convincing?
10. How are the principal characters differentiated during the scene?
11. What is the importance of the smugging episode in *A Portrait?*
12. How is the injustice of Dolan and Arnall portrayed during the pandying of Stephen?
13. What are Stephen's motives in his decision to appeal to Conmee?
14. What details does Joyce use to capture Stephen's fear in the confrontation with the rector?
15. How is Conmee contrasted with Dolan and Arnall?
16. Why does Joyce picture Conmee as sympathetic to Stephen's plight?

17. Describe the "inflation" at the end of Chapter One.
18. Why, symbolically, does Stephen choose to wriggle free from the embrace of his classmates?
19. What is the importance of the "bowl" at the end of Chapter One? Where is the image later found?
20. What is Stephen's attitude towards Dolan after his "victory" over the school disciplinarian?

Chapter Two.

1. Describe the "deflated" beginning of Chapter Two.
2. How are Uncle Charles and Mike Flynn typical of Ireland's "paralyzed" citizens?
3. How does Stephen differ in his aspirations from Aubrey Mills and his other friends?
4. What is the importance of Stephen's "vision" of Mercedes?
5. How does the economic situation of Stephen's family contribute to his depression?
6. What, specifically, is Stephen's attitude towards Dublin?
7. Show how *one* of the four vignettes serves to describe Stephen's personality.
8. How do Stephen's poems to E— C— typify his innocence?
9. Why does Joyce treat almost parenthetically Simon's revelation that the priests at Clongowes looked upon Stephen's protest to Conmee as a joke?
10. Why is the setting for Simon's remarks in the episode significant?
11. Why, symbolically, does Stephen's "play" take place during Whitsuntide?
12. How does the theatre here foreshadow other theatres in the novel?
13. In what sense is Stephen still a "farcical pedagogue" during the play?
14. Describe in detail how Stephen differs from Heron.
15. What is the importance of the "heresy" in Stephen's essay?
16. How is Stephen's defense of Byron both heroic and immature? What is foreshadowed by Stephen's refusal to "admit?"

17. What is the importance of Stephen's perception of the word, "Foetus"?
18. What is Stephen's exact attitude towards his father after the trip to Cork?
19. How does the trip to Cork lead to Stephen's visit with the prostitute?
20. Describe in detail how Stephen's visit compares and contrasts with his "meetings" with other women in *A Portrait*.

Chapter Three.

1. How does the reader's judgment of Stephen's guilt contrast with the protagonist's own estimate of his depleted spiritual state.
2. How is Stephen set apart from the other boys making the retreat?
3. How does Joyce evoke Stephen's feelings that Arnall is speaking directly to him?
4. Why, symbolically, is Arnall the one to conduct the retreat?
5. Why is it dedicated to St. Francis Xavier?
6. How does Arnall reveal his own neurotic personality in his sermons?
7. Discuss several contradictions in Arnall's picture of God. What other blunders does he make?
8. What specific three means does Arnall use to present his picture of Hell?
9. Discuss some of Arnall's vivid details in his description of the Inferno.
10. How do Stephen's feelings after the sermons on Hell parallel his desperation in Cork?
11. Discuss in detail Stephen's dream of the goatish creatures.
12. Once he decides to confess how does Stephen try to alter his attitude towards others?
13. What details indicate Stephen's fears just before the actual confession?
14. Describe in detail Stephen's reception of Penance from the Capuchin. What type of person is the old priest?
15. Where does a reference to Capuchins appear later in the novel?

16. What is the meaning of the color white following Stephen's Confession?
17. How does Stephen feel about Emma after his shriving?
18. What is the importance of Stephen's meal following his reception of Communion?
19. Describe Stephen's "inflation" at the end of the chapter.
20. What is the symbolic importance of the ciborium?

Chapter Four.

1. How do Stephen's reflections on religious matters suggest that his conversion is merely mechanical?
2. How does Joyce satirize Stephen in the opening pages of Chapter Four?
3. How is Stephen's new maturity seen in his meeting with the Director?
4. Discuss in detail the levels of symbolism found in the scene.
5. What reasons does Stephen have for seriously considering ordination?
6. How does Stephen's return to his family's house contrast with the "temptation" offered by the Director in the previous scene?
7. What "epiphany" does Stephen experience when he hears his siblings singing Thomas Moore's lyrics?
8. Why does Stephen pace between Byron's publichouse and Clontarf Chapel (of all places!) before undergoing his illumination?
9. What is the importance of Stephen's sighting a "squad" of Christian Brothers?
10. Why is Stephen called "Bous Stephanoumenos"?
11. Why does Stephen reject the world of the nude, swimming youngsters?
12. In the episode, how does Stephen's namesake, Daedalus, help the protagonist to define his role in life? Discuss the meaning of "fabulous artificer."
13. Discuss the religious imagery at the end of Chapter Four, especially Joyce's allusions to Christ's Resurrection.
14. What Biblical parallel is seen in Stephen's vision of the bird-girl?

15. Apart from the Biblical, what other levels of symbolism does the bird-girl encompass?

16. In what sense is the bird-girl all the women in the novel included in one person?

17. Why does Stephen turn away from her?

18. Describe the "inflation" at the end of the chapter. How does it differ from Stephen's moment of exaltation after the retreat?

19. After rejecting the Church, what type of life, specifically, does Stephen wish to escape into?

20. Is the language in the last part of Chapter Four merely "literary," i.e., without substance? Discuss.

Chapter Five.

1. Describe the deflating effect of Stephen's home at the start of the chapter.

2. Locate elements of the Holy Week Services in the opening pages of Chapter Five.

3. What aspects of Ireland does the woman in Davin's tale represent?

4. In what sense is Stephen's victory over the Dean of Studies a linguistic triumph?

5. What warning does the Dean give Stephen?

6. How are Moynihan and MacAlister differentiated during the lesson in physics?

7. What is the importance here of the "theatre" setting?

8. Why does Stephen refuse to sign MacCann's petition?

9. From which "nets" does Stephen feel he must escape?

10. How does Joyce try to attain dramatic interest during Stephen's discussion of aesthetics?

11. Describe Aquinas' three characteristics of beauty.

12. Distinguish between "lyric," "epic," and "dramatic."

13. Analyze the villanelle as a poem. What is its artistic worth?

14. What does Stephen's composition of the villanelle tell us about him as a person and as an incipient artist?

15. How does Stephen's vision of birds confirm him as a prophet?

16. Why does Joyce portray Cranly as a Confessor?

17. Discuss the "chance" that Stephen feels he is taking by not receiving Communion during the Easter time.

18. What is the importance of Stephen's "spring" diary?
19. In what sense is Cranly Stephen's Precursor?
20. Upon whom does Stephen call at the end of *A Portrait*? Why?

Larger Topics of Discussion

1. Discuss in detail the appropriateness of the title to *A Portrait of the Artist as a Young Man.*

2. Summarize your views of Stephen Dedalus in a lengthy paragraph; then go on to cite individual scenes which express his personality. Try to define the degree of irony in each.

3. Show how individual chapters and parts of chapters follow a technique of "inflation" and "deflation" in delineating the ups and downs of Stephen's changing personality. Does he ever reach "stasis"?

4. Define "epiphany," and try to locate possible epiphanies in the novel. Describe the degree of wisdom (if any) that Stephen gains from each.

5. Why does Joyce compare Stephen throughout *A Portrait* to Byron, St. Francis Xavier, and Lucifer?

6. Is the comparison of Stephen to Christ in *A Portrait* simply ironic? If not, what use do the allusions serve?

7. Do some research into the legend of Daedalus, and cite parallels between the myth and Stephen's portrait.

8. Examine Stephen's changing attitudes towards the priests in *A Portrait*. Do his later feelings regarding them show any maturity?

9. Discuss in detail the reasons that Stephen leaves the Church.

10. Trace the religious symbolism of the several meals mentioned in *A Portrait*.

11. Discuss Joyce's use of bird symbolism in the novel. Does the imagery serve a valid artistic purpose, or is it merely trickery?

12. Tabulate the appearances of water in *A Portrait*, and try to arrive at an exact statement concerning Joyce's use of this symbol.

13. Relate any *one* scene—symbolically, thematically, and architectonically—to the overall novel.

14. In what ways do the opening two pages of *A Portrait* form a microcosm of the novel? Explain how the cuckolding of Stephen (baby tuckoo) throughout the novel is foreshadowed in its first two pages.

15. Is Stephen's composition of the villanelle an asset or a debit in *A Portrait?*

16. Show how Joyce clearly distinguishes among Stephen's companions at the university.

"Outside" Work

1. Describe in detail the character of Simon Dedalus. In what sense is he Stephen's "real" father, even though the protagonist rejects him? Compare the partially mitigating treatment that James Joyce affords Simon with the devastating picture of him given by Stanislaus Joyce in the *Complete Dublin Diary*.

2. Relying upon Ellmann's biography, discuss ways in which Joyce altered the facts of his life to develop the character of Stephen.

3. Read *Stephen Hero* to determine why *A Portrait* is an enduring classic and the early work, a bit of ephemera.

4. Analyze Joyce's early essay, "A Portrait of the Artist" (included in Anderson), in relation to Joyce's novel. Which ideas did Joyce carry over to *A Portrait?* Which did he abandon?

ANNOTATED BIBLIOGRAPHY

Basic Resources

THE TEXT

A Portrait of the Artist as a Young Man: Text, Criticism, and Notes, ed. Chester G. Anderson. New York: Viking Press, Viking Critical Library, 1968. This is the text used in the present commentary on *A Portrait.* Anderson's edition is authoritative, and the critical readings at the back of the text are indispensable to the beginning student of Joyce; they contain selections from the chief critical writings on *A Portrait.* The scholarship deals with such controversial issues as Joyce's aesthetic distance and his use of irony in *A Portrait* and tries to situate the book in the literary tradition of the novel. Interesting, too, is Anderson's inclusion of contemporary reactions to *A Portrait.*

JOYCE'S LETTERS

The Letters of James Joyce: Volume One, ed. Stuart Gilbert. New York: Viking Pres, 1957. New edition with corrections, 1966. *Volumes Two and Three,* ed. Richard Ellmann. New York: Viking Press, 1966. Frequently, Joyce felt compelled to explain his literary intentions through letters; and, though many of the missives deal with trivia, some contain fine insight into Joyce's writing methods. Ellmann's index at the end of the third volume is especially helpful.

BIOGRAPHY

Ellmann, Richard. *James Joyce.* New York: Oxford University Press, 1959. Ellmann's work is the definitive biography of Joyce; readable and complete, *James Joyce* won the 1959 National Book Award for nonfiction. Ellmann excels in combining the facts of Joyce's life with his fictional treatment of Stephen Dedalus. About Stephen, Ellmann writes, "Of this young man it may be safely predicted that he will write letters home." According to Ellmann, Joyce's favorite characters are those "who in one way or another retreat before masculinity, yet are loved regardless by motherly women."

BIBLIOGRAPHY

Beebe, Maurice, Phillip F. Herring, and Walton Litz. "Criticism of James Joyce: A Selected Checklist." *Modern Fiction Studies*, XV (Spring 1969), 105-82. Although selective, the checklist provides a sound beginning guide to scholarship on *A Portrait*.

CASEBOOKS

Connolly, Thomas E., ed. *Joyce's Portrait: Criticisms and Critiques*. New York: Appleton-Century-Crofts, 1962; Morris, William E., and Clifford A. Nault, Jr., eds. *Portraits of an Artist: A Casebook on James Joyce's A Portrait of the Artist as a Young Man*. New York: Odyssey Press, 1962; and Schutte, W.M., ed. *Twentieth Century Interpretations of A Portrait of the Artist as a Young Man*. Englewood Cliffs, New Jersey: Prentice-Hall, 1968. All three of the casebooks contain valuable information on *A Portrait*—although the articles overlap. In the present analysis, only those articles *not* included in the casebooks or in Anderson's Critical Edition of *A Portrait* are listed in the section of the Annotated Bibliography dealing with *A Portrait*. Almost one half of Connolly's casebook is devoted to articles concerned with Stephen's aesthetic theory; Morris and Nault offer a thought provoking final summary of topics for further research, and their book includes John V. Kelleher's "The Perceptions of James Joyce"; and Schutte's collection contains the perceptive comments of Wayne C. Booth in "The Problem of Distance in *A Portrait of the Artist*."

THE JAMES JOYCE QUARTERLY

From its inception, the *JJQ* has provided the best of new thinking on Joyce's work through its willingness to publish beginning scholars as well as established Joyceans. Each year the Journal publishes a supplemental list of Joyce criticism sometimes not found in the *PMLA Annual Bibliography,* and the editor's Preface to each issue both provides the "flavor" of contemporary Joyceana and points out new works on Joyce. The summer issue in 1967 was devoted to *A Portrait* and contains important comments by Kain, Feshbach, Naremore, Magalaner, and several others.

General Works on Joyce

Burgess, Anthony. *RE JOYCE.* New York: Norton, 1965. Published in England as *Here Comes Everybody: An Introduction to James Joyce for the Ordinary Reader.* London: Faber, 1965. Burgess provides a sound introduction to Joyce's works, and, through his novelist's point-of-view, offers many untraditional insights into *A Portrait.* As does Ellmann, Burgess sees gestation as a central image in the novel: in Chapter One, for example, "The embryonic soul is surrounded by a sort of amniotic fluid—urine and the sea . . . " Spending a full section of his book on Chapter Five of *A Portrait,* Burgess finds that Stephen's aesthetic theory is "delivered with such brilliant eloquence that it reminds us of another lengthy and authoritative piece of propaganda—Father Arnall's sermon on hell, which this peripatetic discourse exactly balances."

Cixous, Hélène. *L'Exil de James Joyce, ou l'art du remplacement.* Paris: Grasset, 1968. Ms. Cixous' book is lengthy and cumbersome but does offer some insights into Joyce's work. The tome is worth looking into, particularly if one is not bothered by the occasional mistranslations of Joyce's words.

Deming, Robert H., ed. *James Joyce: The Critical Heritage,* 2 vols. New York: Barnes & Noble, 1970. Deming includes many interesting contemporary reactions to *A Portrait,* and the study, in two volumes, justifies itself. Early comments show that the world was not entirely unappreciative of Joyce's work.

Epstein, Edmund L. *The Ordeal of Stephen Dedalus: The Conflict of Generations in James Joyce's A Portrait of the Artist as a Young Man.* Carbondale: Southern Illinois University Press, 1971. Epstein presents a well-reasoned analysis of the father-son conflict in Joyce. Eschewing recent psychoanalytical portraits of Joyce's characters, Epstein traces through Joyce's works the image of King David, messiah and writer.

Hodgart, Matthew J.C., and Mabel Worthington. *Song in the Works of James Joyce.* New York: Columbia University Press, 1959. A classic book on Joyce, the Hodgart and Worthington volume is a through analysis of the music that Joyce alluded to from the beginning to the end of his works. The authors' study of references to songs which influenced Joyce illuminates hundreds of otherwise opaque passages in Joyce's books.

James Joyce Review, ed. Edmund L. Epstein. Vol. I, no. 1 (Feb. 2, 1957) to Vol. III, no. 1-2 (1959). During its brief lifetime, Epstein's journal published several important pieces on Joyce.

Kenner, Hugh. *Dublin's Joyce.* Bloomington: Indiana University Press, 1956. Kenner's book contains his revised version of the famous essay, *"The Portrait in Perspective,"* which appeared originally in *James Joyce: Two Decades of Criticism,* ed. Seon Givens. New York: Vanguard Press, 1948, with enlarged edition, 1963. Kenner's work is mandatory reading for an intelligent approach to *A Portrait.* Especially valuable is his analysis of similarities between *A Portrait* and *Ulysses* and *Finnegans Wake.* In addition, Kenner demonstrates a "precise analogical structure" which suggests that the "action of each of the five chapters is really the same action. The pattern of dream nourished in contempt of reality, put into practice, and dashed by reality, is worked out in the five chapters in five main modes, and in numerous subordinate instances." Kenner depicts Stephen's unsympathetic nature in Chapter Five by a close analysis of symbols and thematic parallels.

Levin, Harry. *James Joyce: A Critical Introduction.* Norfolk: New Directions, 1941. Rev. ed., 1960. Levin stresses Joyce's vivid use of conversation in *A Portrait*, relating Simon Dedalus, for example, to Sean O'Casey's "Paycock": "with all his amiable failings, he is Ireland itself."

Litz, Walton. *James Joyce.* Twayne's English Authors Series, 31. New York: Twayne Publishers, 1966. This is a compact study of Joyce by a leading Joycean. Of *A Portrait*, Litz writes, "We see Stephen as a sterile egotist, cut off from humanity by his lonely pride; yet we also appreciate his imaginative powers, and sympathize with his plight."

Magalaner, Marvin. *Time of Apprenticeship: The Fiction of Young James Joyce.* New York: Abelard-Schuman, 1959. This is an excellent appraisal of the young man who went on to write *Ulysses* and *Finnegans Wake.*

—————, ed. *A James Joyce Miscellany.* New York: James Joyce Society, 1957.

—————, ed. *A James Joyce Miscellany: Second Series.* Carbondale: Southern Illinois University Press, 1959.

—————, ed. *A James Joyce Miscellany: Third Series.* Carbondale: Southern Illinois University Press, 1962. Especially relevant to *A Portrait* are two essays from the Second Series: Maurice Beebe's "Joyce and Stephen Dedalus: The Problem of Autobiography" and Adaline Glasheen's "Joyce and the Three Ages of Charles Stewart Parnell"; and one essay from the Third Series: James R. Thrane's "Joyce's Sermon on Hell." Beebe feels that in *A Portrait* Joyce developed "the image of an archetypal artist, gave it the appropriately symbolic name of 'Dedalus,' and carefully removed from the composite figure any traits of his own character that conflicted with the stereotype." Ms. Glasheen traces the background of the Parnell scandal in *A Portrait*. Thrane discusses many parallels between Pinamonti's *Hell Opened to Christians* and Father Arnall's sermons.

——————, and Richard M. Kain. *Joyce: The Man, the Work, the Reputation*. New York: New York University Press, 1956. An indispensable assessment of Joyce's stature.

Morse, J. Mitchell. *The Sympathetic Alien: James Joyce and Catholicism*. New York: New York University Press, 1959. Morse's widely read book is in part an attempt to define Joyce's feelings towards his religious upbringing. Morse writes, "Thus Joyce's final attitude toward the Jesuits is ... ambivalent; for though if he is to function as an artist he must struggle free of their moral grip, he must also as an artist take them into account, not merely as straw men to be knocked down ... but as representatives of an attitude that does a great deal to make human life what it is."

Moseley, Virginia. *Joyce and the Bible*. DeKalb: Northern Illinois University Press, 1967. Ms. Moseley's book is provocative, though at times overly ingenious. For example, her parallel between the Christmas Dinner Scene and the debate of the twelve year old Christ in the Temple distorts Stephen's age in *A Portrait*. Moseley's book, on the whole, however, is well worth reading.

Noon, William T., S.J. *Joyce and Aquinas*. Yale University Press, 1957. By pointing out the shallowness of Stephen's grasp of Aquinas, Father Noon helps to place *A Portrait* in true perspective. Less convincing is Noon's view that the Retreat Sermon is a gross exaggeration of Catholic practices. Scholarly and well-reasoned, Noon's book is a landmark in Joycean commentary—in spite of its over emphasis on Joyce's Thomistic lacunae.

O'Brien, Darcy. *The Conscience of James Joyce*. Princeton University Press, 1967. O'Brien successfuly illustrates his thesis that Joyce's comedy stems from his moral sense: "For all his literary experiments and innovations, he retained a vision of human frailty closer in spirit to his Irish Catholic background than to the moral relativism characteristic of our age."

Staley, Thomas F., ed. *James Joyce Today: Essays on the Major Works*, Bloomington: Indiana University Press, 1966. This book contains Noon's "A Portrait of the Artist as a Young Man: After Fifty Years," which touches on many aspects of the novel including its homosexual overtones. About *A Portrait*, Noon writes, "And how might any story both of the loss of faith and the search for faith grow irrelevant in the twentieth century?"

Strong, L.A.G. *The Sacred River: An Approach to James Joyce*. New York: Pellegrini and Cudahy, 1951. Strong's work is an important early study of religious symbolism in Joyce.

Tindall, William York. *James Joyce: His Way of Interpreting the Modern World*. New York: Scribners, 1950.

——————. *A Reader's Guide to James Joyce*. New York: Noonday Press, 1959. Both books are crucial, revealing Tindall's extraordinary insight into Joyce's use of symbols.

Biographical Sources

Anderson, Chester G. *James Joyce and His World*. New York: Viking Press, 1968. Anderson interestingly combines biographical facts with his own imaginings in telling Joyce's story through well over a hundred photographs.

Byrne, J.F. *Silent Years: An Autobiography, with Memoirs of James Joyce and Our Ireland*. New York: Farrar, Straus, and Young, 1953. Byrne's book contains a good deal of information on Joyce by "Cranly," of *A Portrait*, though much of the work is taken up with trivial events of Byrne's own life. Byrne, not having "made it," as Joyce did, has his ax to grind.

Colum, Mary and Padraic. *Our Friend James Joyce*. Garden City, N.Y.: Doubleday, 1958. The Colums, acquaintances of Joyce, provide important information concerning religious aspects of Joyce's life.

Curran, Constantine. *James Joyce Remembered*. New York: Oxford University Press, 1968. Despite minor flaws in scholarship, this book by a lifelong friend of Joyce offers excellent documentation of influences on Joyce and helps to balance Joyce's overly pessimistic picture of the Dublin of his youth.

Edel, Leon. *James Joyce: The Last Journey*. New York: Gotham Book Mart, 1947. Edel's book is a moving account of Joyce's last days.

Gorman, Herbert. *James Joyce*. New York: Rinehart, 1940; rev. ed. 1948. Gorman's book is an obviously important biographical source, though one partially inspired by a Joyce who was gazing through the haze of nostalgia and who exaggerated the negative aspects of his youth.

Joyce, Stanislaus. *The Complete Dublin Diary of Stanislaus Joyce*, ed. George H. Healey. Ithaca, N.Y. Cornell University Press, 1971.

——. *My Brother's Keeper: James Joyce's Early Years*, ed. Richard Ellmann. Preface by T.S. Eliot. New York: Viking Press, 1958. Although these works by Joyce's brother treat the days of their youth with excessive bitterness, they are indispensable to an understanding of the early influences—especially religious ones—

upon James Joyce. The Complete Diary was written, in Dublin, between 1903 and 1905 and includes thirty-six additional pages of manuscript once suppressed.

Sullivan, Kevin. *Joyce among the Jesuits.* New York: Columbia University Press, 1958. Sullivan's analysis of the religious influences on Joyce during his schooldays dispels many false notions. Sullivan informs us that Joyce "was an exceptional schoolboy of proved scholastic superiority, of sound if fragile health, and, to all outward appearances, of substantial moral and religious disposition. As such, he had all the physical, intellectual, and moral qualities prerequisite for a vocation to the priesthood."

Criticism Specific to "A Portrait"

Atherton, James, ed. *A Portrait of the Artist as a Young Man.* London: Heinemann Educational Books, Ltd., 1964. Atherton's introduction to the edition and his notes, which point out several overlooked sources of Joyce's work, are especially helpful.

August, Eugene R. "Father Arnall's Use of Scripture in *A Portrait.*" *James Joyce Quarterly,* IV (Summer 1967), 275-79. Speaking of the retreat master in *A Portrait* and the author of *Hell Opened to Christians,* August states, "When Joyce set about writing Father Arnall's sermons, not only did he have Arnall borrow Pinamonti's words, but he also had the Irish priest commit the Italian priest's mistakes."

Beja, Morris, ed. *James Joyce, Dubliners and A Portrait of the Artist as a Young Man: A Selection of Critical Essays.* London: Macmillan, 1973. This volume contains important comments on Joyce's early works.

Doherty, James. "Joyce and *Hell Opened to Christians:* The Edition He Used for His Hell Sermons." *Modern Philology,* LXI (November, 1963), 110-119. Doherty analyzes the use to which Joyce put Pinamonti in

writing the retreat sermons: "Most of the changes in
the text are similar to what Joyce did with the description of organs burning in the body: a sharpening up of
the language where the original is vague."

Harrison, Kate. "The *Portrait* Epiphany." *James Joyce
Quarterly*, VIII (Winter 1971), 142-50. In omitting
explicit mention of the Epiphany in *A Portrait*, Stephen "effectively excludes the implications of deter-
minism which are intrinsic to the epiphany . . . "

Jones, David E. "The Essence of Beauty in James Joyce's
Aesthetics." *James Joyce Quarterly*, X (Spring 1973),
291-311. Jones' study of the influence of Aristotle and
Aquinas on Stephen's theory of art is lucid and detailed.

Modern Fiction Studies, XV (Spring 1969). This issue is a
special James Joyce number.

Reddick, Bryan. "The Importance of Tone in the Structural Rhythm of Joyce's *Portrait*." *James Joyce Quarterly*, VI (Spring 1969), 201-18. Reddick presents a
thoughtful "general study of the relation between
variations in tone and the structure of *A Portrait* . . . "
At the start of Chapter Five, for example, "It is not
just . . . the prosaic subject matter here, but also the
'prosaic' treatment of it, which qualifies the emotion
of the earlier passage."

Ryf, Robert S. *A New Approach to Joyce: A Portrait of
the Artist as a Guidebook*. University of California
Press, 1962. Ryf's thesis is interesting: "all Joyce's
themes are present in the *Portrait*, and his major
techniques are present, at least in embryo. . . . I offer
my personal opinion . . . that the *Portrait* is esthetically
the most pleasing and therefore, in a sense, the best-
written of his works."

Scholes, Robert. "Joyce and the Epiphany: The Key to the
Labyrinth?" *Sewanee Review*, LXXII (Jan.-March,
1964), 65-77. Scholes writes of the Epiphany, "As a

term to be used in the criticism of Joyce's art itself,
I would like to see it abandoned entirely."

Scholes, Robert, and Richard M. Kain, eds. *The Workshop
of Daedalus: James Joyce and the Materials for A Portrait of the Artist as a Young Man.* Evanston, Ill.:
Northwestern University Press, 1965. This is a
thorough study of the raw materials which went into
A Portrait, with an analysis of biographical facts.

Scotto, Robert M. " 'Visions' and 'Epiphanies' : Fictional
Technique in Pater's *Marius* and Joyce's *Portrait."
James Joyce Quarterly,* XI (Fall 1973), 41-50. Scotto
traces several parallels between Walter Pater's use of
"visions" in *Marius the Epicurean* (1885) and Joyce's
Epiphanies in *A Portrait.* Scotto finds, for example,
"Sight leads to 'vision' . . . for religion comes to both
Pater and Joyce through the senses, especially the
optical."

Staley, Thomas F. *A Critical Study Guide to James Joyce's
A Portrait of the Artist as a Young Man.* Totowa, N.J.:
Littlefield, Adams, 1968. Staley's comments form a
sound, competent introduction to Joyce's novel.

Walsh, Ruth M. "That Pervasive Mass—In *Dubliners* and
*A Portrait of the Artist as a Young Man." James Joyce
Quarterly,* VIII (Spring 1971), 205-220. Ms. Walsh
maintains that there are no close, one-to-one parallels
between parts of the Mass and the organization of
A Portrait: "Yes, there is a Maundy Thursday mass in
the fifth chapter of *Portrait,* but Joyce incorporated
it far more symbolically than structurally."

NOTES

NOTES

NOTES

NOTES

NOTES

NOTES

NOTES

NOTES

NOTES

NOTES

NOTES

NOTES

NOTES

NOTES

MONARCH® NOTES AND STUDY GUIDES

ARE AVAILABLE AT RETAIL STORES EVERYWHERE

In the event your local bookseller cannot provide you with other Monarch titles you want—

ORDER ON THE FORM BELOW:

Complete order form appears on inside front & back covers for your convenience.

Simply send retail price, local sales tax, if any, plus 25¢ to cover mailing & handling.

IBM #	AUTHOR & TITLE (exactly as shown on title listing)	PRICE
	PLUS ADD'L FOR POSTAGE	25¢
	GRAND TOTAL	

MONARCH® PRESS, a division of Simon & Schuster, Inc.
Mail Service Department, 1 West 39th Street, New York, N.Y. 10018

I enclose................................. dollars to cover retail price, local sales tax, plus mailing and handling.

Name_____
(Please print)

Address_____

City_____ State_____ Zip_____

Please send check or money order. We cannot be responsible for cash.